Chaosmosis

an ethico-aesthetic paradigm

To DBH,

Best wishes for 2025

Chaosmosis

an ethico-aesthetic paradigm

Félix Guattari

translated by

Paul Bains and Julian Pefanis

POWER PUBLICATIONS

SYDNEY

This translation was assisted by the French Government
through the Ministry for Culture and Communications

Published by
Power Publications
Power Institute of Fine Arts
The University of Sydney
NSW 2006 Australia

General Editor
Julian Pefanis

Managing Editor
Gregory Harvey

Cover design
Aaron Rogers

Printed by
Southwood Press

National Library of Australia Cataloguing-in-publication entry
Guattari, Félix, 1930-
    [Chaosmose. English]. Chaosmosis: an ethico-aesthetic paradigm.

    ISBN 0 909952 25 6.

    1. Psychoanalysis - Philosophy. 2. Subjectivity.
    I. Title. II. Title: Chaosmose. English

150.195

On the planking, on the ship's bulwarks, on the sea, with the course of the sun through the sky and the ship, an unreadable and wrenching script takes shape, takes shape and destroys itself at the same slow pace — shadows, spines, shafts of broken light refocused in the angles, the triangles of a fleeting geometry that yields to the shadow of the ocean waves. And then, unceasingly, lives again.

Marguerite Duras
The North China Lover

The author:
Félix Guattari was a psychoanalyst, philosopher and ecologist, well-known for his collaborative works with Gilles Deleuze (*Anti-Oedipus, A Thousand Plateaus, What is Philosophy*) – considered by many to be among the most significant philosophical texts of the past 50 years. To date, little of his own work has been translated into English (*Molecular Revolution, 1975*). Active in his younger years as a Left wing militant and later as an ecologist, his prime focus was the innovative psychiatric clinic at Le Borde, which he established and where he worked until his death in 1992.

The translators:
Paul Bains is a research academic working in a transdisciplinary field of philosophy and science. He is currently translating a collection of essays by Isabelle Stengers. Julian Pefanis teaches at The University of Sydney. He is author of *Heterology and the Postmodern*, and has translated works by Pierre Clastres, Jean-François Lyotard and Jean Baudrillard.

Contents

1

On the production of subjectivity

My professional activities in the field of psychotherapy, like my political and cultural engagements, have led me increasingly to put the emphasis on subjectivity as the product of individuals, groups and institutions.

Considering subjectivity from the point of view of its production does not imply any return to traditional systems of binary determination — material infrastructure/ideological superstructure. The various semiotic registers that combine to engender subjectivity do not maintain obligatory hierarchical relations fixed for all time. Sometimes, for example, economic semiotisation becomes dependent on collective psychological factors — look at the sensitivity of the stock exchange to fluctuations of opinion. Subjectivity is in fact plural and polyphonic — to use Mikhaïl Bakhtin's expression. It recognises no dominant or determinant instance guiding all other forms according to a univocal causality.

At least three types of problem prompt us to enlarge the definition of subjectivity beyond the classical opposition between individual subject and society, and in so doing, revise the models of the unconscious currently in circulation: the irruption of

subjective factors at the forefront of current events, the massive
development of machinic productions of subjectivity and, finally, the recent prominence of ethological and ecological perspectives on human subjectivity.

Subjective factors have always held an important place in
the course of history. But it seems that with the global diffusion
of the mass media they are beginning to play a dominant role.
We will only give a few brief examples here. The immense
movement unleashed by the Chinese students at Tiananmen
Square obviously had as its goal the slogans of political democ-
ratisation. But it is equally certain that the contagious affective
charges it bore far surpassed simple ideological demands. A
whole lifestyle, collective ethic and conception of social relations (derived largely from Western images) were set into
motion. And in the long run tanks won't be able to stop it! As in
Hungary or Poland, collective existential mutation will have
the last word! All the same, large movements of subjectivation
don't necessarily develop in the direction of emancipation. The
massive subjective revolution which has been developing
among the Iranian people for more than ten years is focused on
religious archaisms and generally conservative social attitudes
— particularly with regard to the position of women (this is a
sensitive issue in France, because of the events in the Maghreb
and the repercussions of these repressive attitudes to women in
the area of immigration).

In the Eastern bloc, the fall of the Iron Curtain didn't happen as the result of armed insurrection but through the crystallisation of an immense collective desire annihilating the
mental substrate of the post-Stalin totalitarian system. This is a
phenomenon of extreme complexity, since it intermingles
emancipatory aspirations with retrogressive, conservative —
even fascist — drives of a nationalistic, ethnic and religious
nature. In this upheaval, how will the populations of central

Europe and the Eastern bloc overcome the bitter deception the capitalist West has reserved for them until now? History will tell us — admittedly a History full of unpleasant surprises but, why not — about a subsequent renewal of social struggles! By contrast, how murderous the Gulf War will have been! One could almost speak of genocide, since this war led to the extermination of many more Iraqis (counting all ethnic groups) than there were victims of the bombs dropped at Hiroshima and Nagasaki in 1945. With the passage of time it seems clear that what was at stake was an attempt to bring the Arab populations to heel and reclaim world opinion: it had to be demonstrated that the Yankee way of subjectivation could be imposed by the combined power of the media and arms.

Generally, one can say that contemporary history is increasingly dominated by rising demands for subjective singularity — quarrels over language, autonomist demands, issues of nationalism and of the nation, which, in total ambiguity, express on the one hand an aspiration for national liberation, but also manifest themselves in what I would call conservative reterritorialisations of subjectivity. A certain universal representation of subjectivity, incarnated by capitalist colonialism in both East and West, has gone bankrupt — although it's not yet possible to fully measure the scale of such a failure. Today, as everyone knows, the growth of nationalism and fundamentalism in Arab and Muslim countries may have incalculable consequences not only on international relations, but on the subjective economies of hundreds of millions of individuals. It's the whole problematic of disarray as well as the mounting demands of the Third World, the countries of the South, which are thus stamped with an agonising question mark.

As things stand, sociology, economic science, political science and legal studies appear poorly equipped to account for

this mixture of archaic attachments to cultural traditions that
nonetheless aspire to the technological and scientific modernity
characterising the contemporary subjective cocktail.
Traditional psychoanalysis, for its part, is hardly better placed
to confront these problems, due to its habit of reducing social
facts to psychological mechanisms. In such conditions it
appears opportune to forge a more transversalist conception of
subjectivity, one which would permit us to understand both its
idiosyncratic territorialised couplings (Existential Territories)
and its opening onto value systems (Incorporeal Universes)
with their social and cultural implications.

Should we keep the semiotic productions of the mass media,
informatics, telematics and robotics separate from psychological
subjectivity? I don't think so. Just as social machines can be
grouped under the general title of Collective Equipment, technological machines of information and communication operate at
the heart of human subjectivity, not only within its memory and
intelligence, but within its sensibility, affects and unconscious
fantasms. Recognition of these machinic dimensions of subjectivation leads us to insist, in our attempt at redefinition, on the
heterogeneity of the components leading to the production of
subjectivity. Thus one finds in it: 1. Signifying semiological components which appear in the family, education, the environment, religion, art, sport ... 2. Elements constructed by the
media industry, the cinema, etc., 3. A-signifying semiological
dimensions that trigger informational sign machines, and that
function in parallel or independently of the fact that they produce and convey significations and denotations, and thus
escape from strictly linguistic axiomatics. The different currents
of structuralism have given neither autonomy nor specificity to
this a-signifying regime, although authors like Julia Kristeva or
Jacques Derrida have shed some light on the relative autonomy
of this sort of component. But in general, the a-signifying econo-

my of language has been reduced to what I call sign machines, to the linguistic, significational economy of language. This tendency is particularly clear with Roland Barthes who equates the elements of language and narrative segments with figures of Expression, and thus confers on linguistic semiology a primacy over all other semiotics. It was a grave error on the part of the structuralist school to try to put everything connected with the psyche under the control of the linguistic signifier! Technological transformations oblige us to be aware of both universalising and reductionist homogenisations of subjectivity and of a heterogenetic tendency, that is to say, of a reinforcement of the heterogeneity and singularisation of its components. Thus "computer-aided design" leads to the production of images opening on to unprecedented plastic Universes — I am thinking, for example, of Matta's work with the graphic palette — or to the solution of mathematical problems which would have been quite unimaginable a few years ago. But then again, we should be on guard against progressivist illusions or visions which are systematically pessimistic. The machinic production of subjectivity can work for the better or for the worse. There exists an anti-modernist attitude which involves a massive rejection of technological innovation, particularly as it concerns the information revolution. It's impossible to judge such a machinic evolution either positively or negatively; everything depends on its articulation within collective assemblages of enunciation. At best there is the creation, or invention, of new Universes of reference; at the worst there is the deadening influence of the mass media to which millions of individuals are currently condemned. Technological developments together with social experimentation in these new domains are perhaps capable of leading us out of the current period of oppression and into a post-media era characterised by the reappropriation and resingularisation of the use of media. (Access to data-banks, video libraries, interactivity between participants, etc.)

The same movement towards a polyphonic and heterogenetic comprehension of subjectivity leads us to consider certain aspects of contemporary research into ethology and ecology. Daniel Stern, in *The Interpersonal World of the Infant*,[1] has notably explored the pre-verbal subjective formations of infants. He shows that these are not at all a matter of "stages" in the Freudian sense, but of levels of subjectivation which maintain themselves in parallel throughout life. He thus rejects the overrated psychogenesis of Freudian complexes, which have been presented as the structural "Universals" of subjectivity. Furthermore, he emphasises the inherently trans-subjective character of an infant's early experiences, which do not dissociate the feeling of self from the feeling of the other. A dialectic between "sharable affects" and "non-sharable affects" thus structures the emergent phases of subjectivity. A nascent subjectivity, which we will continually find in dreams, *délire*, creative exaltation, or the feeling of love...

Social ecology and mental ecology have found privileged sites of exploration in the experiences of institutional psychotherapy. I am obviously thinking of the clinic at La Borde, where I have worked for a long time; everything there is set up so that psychotic patients live in a climate of activity and assume responsibility, not only with the goal of developing an ambience of communication, but also in order to create local centres for collective subjectivation. Thus it's not simply a matter of remodelling a patient's subjectivity — as it existed before a psychotic crisis — but of a production *sui generis*. For example, certain psychotic patients, coming from poor agricultural backgrounds, will be invited to take up plastic arts, drama, video, music, etc., whereas until then, these universes had been unknown to them. On the other hand, bureaucrats and intellectuals will find themselves attracted to material work, in the kitchen, garden, pottery, horse riding club. The important thing here is not only the confrontation with a new material of expression, but the constitution of complexes of subjectivation: multiple exchanges between individual-group-machine. These complexes actually offer people diverse possibilities for recomposing their existential corporeality, to get out of their repetitive impasses and, in a certain way, to resingularise themselves. Grafts of transference operate in this way, not issuing from ready-made dimensions of subjectivity crystallised into structural complexes, but from a creation which itself indicates a kind of aesthetic paradigm. One creates new modalities of subjectivity in the same way that an artist creates new forms from the palette. In such a context, the most heterogeneous components may work towards a patient's positive evolution: relations with architectural space; economic relations; the co-management by patient and carer of the different vectors of treatment; taking advantage of all occasions opening onto the outside world; a processual exploitation of event-centred "singularities" — everything which can contribute to the creation of an authentic relation with the other. To each of these components of the caring institution there corresponds a necessary practice. We are not confronted with a subjectivity given as in-itself, but with processes of the realisation of autonomy, or of autopoiesis (in a somewhat different sense from the one Francisco Varela gives this term[2]).

Let us now examine an example of the use of the psyche's ethological and ecological resources in the domain of family psychotherapy. We are borrowing this example from a movement which, around Mony Elkaim, is attempting to free itself from the grip of systemic theories that circulate in Anglo-Saxon countries and in Italy.[3] Here also the inventiveness of treatment distances us from scientific paradigms and brings us closer to an ethico-aesthetic paradigm. Therapists get involved, take risks and put their own fantasms into operation, creating a paradoxical climate of existential authenticity accompanied by a playful freedom and simulacra. Family therapy produces subjectivity in the most artificial way imaginable. This can be observed during training sessions, when the therapists improvise psychodramatic scenes. Here, the scene implies a layering of enunciation: a vision of oneself as concrete embodiment; a subject of enunciation which doubles the subject of the statement and the distribution of roles; a collective management of the game; an interlocution with observers commenting on the scene; and finally, video which through *feedback* restores the totality of these superposed levels. This type of performance favours the relinquishment of a "realist" attitude which would apprehend the lived scenes as actually embodied in family structures. This multi-faceted theatrical aspect allows us to grasp the artificial and creative character of the production of subjectivity. It should be emphasised that the video is always within sight of the therapists. Even when the camera is switched off, they develop the habit of observing certain semiotic manifestations which would escape normal observation. The ludic face-to-face encounter with patients and the acceptance of singularities developed in this sort of therapy distinguishes it from the attitude of the traditional psychoanalyst with an averted gaze, and even from classical psychodrama.

Whether one considers contemporary history, machinic semiotic productions, the ethology of infancy, or social and mental ecology, we witness the same questioning of subjective individuation, which certainly survives, but is wrought by collective assemblages of enunciation. At this stage, the provisional definition of subjectivity I would like to propose as the most encompassing would be: "The ensemble of conditions which render possible the emergence of individual and/or collective instances as self-referential existential Territories, adjacent, or in a delimiting relation, to an alterity that is itself subjective." We know that in certain social and semiological contexts, subjectivity becomes individualised; persons, taken as responsible for themselves, situate themselves within relations of alterity governed by familial habits, local customs, juridical laws, etc. In other conditions, subjectivity is collective — which does not, however, mean that it becomes exclusively social. The term "collective" should be understood in the sense of a multiplicity that deploys itself as much beyond the individual, on the side of the socius, as before the person, on the side of preverbal intensities, indicating a logic of affects rather than a logic of delimited sets.

The conditions of production sketched out in this redefinition thus together imply: human inter-subjective instances manifested by language; suggestive and identificatory examples from ethology; institutional interactions of different natures; machinic apparatuses (for example, those involving computer technology); incorporeal Universes of reference such as those relative to music and the plastic arts. This non-human pre-personal part of subjectivity is crucial since it is from this that its heterogenesis can develop. It would be to misjudge Deleuze and Foucault — who emphasised the non-human part of subjectivity — to suspect them of taking anti-humanist positions! That's not the issue. Rather, it's a question of being aware of the existence of machines of subjectivation which don't simply work within the "the faculties of the soul," interpersonal relations or intra-familial complexes. Subjectivity does not only produce itself through the psychogenetic stages of psychoanalysis or the "mathemes" of the Unconscious, but also in the large-scale social machines of language and the mass media— which cannot be described as human. A certain bal-

ance still needs to be struck between structuralist discoveries —
which are certainly not unimportant — and their pragmatic
application, so as not to flounder in the social abandon of post-
modernism.

With his concept of the Unconscious Freud postulated the
existence of a hidden continent of the psyche, where instinctu-
al, affective and cognitive options are in large part would be
played out. Today we can't dissociate the theories of the
Unconscious from the psychoanalytic, psychotherapeutic,
institutional and literary practices which make reference to it.
The Unconscious has become an institution, "Collective
Equipment" understood in a broadest sense. One finds oneself
rigged out with an unconscious the moment one dreams,
délires, forgets or makes a slip of the tongue ... Freudian discoveries — which I prefer to call inventions — have undoubtedly
enriched the ways we can approach the psyche. I am certainly
not speaking pejoratively of invention! In the same way that
Christians invented a new form of subjectivation (courtly
chivalry and romanticism, a new love, a new nature) and
Bolshevism a new sense of class, the various Freudian sects
have secreted new ways of experiencing — or even of producing — hysteria, infantile neurosis, psychosis, family conflict,
the reading of myths, etc. The Freudian Unconscious has itself
evolved in the course of its history: it has lost the seething richness and disquieting atheism of its origins and, in its structuralist version, has been recentered on the analysis of the self, its
adaptation to society, and its conformity with a signifying
order.

My perspective involves shifting the human and social sciences
from scientific paradigms towards ethico-aesthetic paradigms.
It's no longer a question of determining whether the Freudian
Unconscious or the Lacanian Unconscious provide scientific

answers to the problems of the psyche. From now on these
models, along with the others, will only be considered in terms
of the production of subjectivity — inseparable as much from
the technical and institutional apparatuses which promote it as
from their impact on psychiatry, university teaching or the
mass media ... In a more general way, one has to admit that
every individual and social group conveys its own system of
modelising subjectivity; that is, a certain cartography — composed of cognitive references as well as mythical, ritual and
symptomatological references — with which it positions itself
in relation to its affects and anguishes, and attempts to manage
its inhibitions and drives.

Psychoanalytic treatment confronts us with a multiplicity
of cartographies: that of the analyst and analysand, and of the
family, the neighbourhood, etc. It is the interaction of these
cartographies that will provide regimes to the different assemblages of subjectivation. None of them, whether fantasmatic,
delirious or theoretical, can be said to express an objective
knowledge of the psyche. All of them are important insofar as
they support a certain context, a certain framework, an existential armature of the subjective situation. Our question here
is not simply of a speculative order, but is posed in very practical ways: how appropriate are concepts of the Unconcious,
offered to us on the psychoanalytic "market," to actual conditions of the production of subjectivity? Should they be trans-
formed, should new ones be invented? This question of modelisation (more exactly of psychological metamodelisation) leads
to an evaluation of the usefulness of these cartographic instruments — these concepts from psychoanalysis, systems theory,
etc. Do we use them as a grid for an exclusive universal reading, with scientific claims, or as partial instruments, in combi-
nation with others, the ultimate criterion being of a functional
order? What processes unfold in a consciousness affected by

the shock of the unexpected? How can a mode of thought, a
capacity to apprehend, be modified when the surrounding
world itself is in the throes of change ? How are the representations of an exterior world changed when it is itself in the
process of changing? The Freudian Unconscious is inseparable
from a society attached to its past, to its phallocratic traditions
and subjective invariants. Contemporary upheavals undoubtedly call for a modelisation turned more towards the future and
the emergence of new social and aesthetic practices. The deval-
uation of the meaning of life provokes the fragmentation of the
self-image: its representations become confused and contradictory. Faced with these upheavals the best attitude would be to
envisage the work of cartography and psychological modelisation in a dialectical relation with the individuals and groups
concerned; the crucial thing is to move in the direction of co-
management in the production of subjectivity, to distrust suggestion and the attitudes of authority which occupy such a
large place in psychoanalysis, in spite of the fact that it claims
to have escaped them.

    A long time ago I renounced the Conscious-Unconscious
dualism of the Freudian topoi and all the Manichean oppositions correlative to Oedipal triangulation and to the castration
complex. I opted for an Unconscious superposing multiple strata of subjectivation, heterogeneous strata of variable extension
and consistency. Thus a more "schizo" Unconscious, one liber-
ated from familial shackles, turned more towards actual praxis
than towards fixations on, and regressions to, the past. An
Unconscious of Flux and of abstract machines rather than an
Unconscious of structure and language. I don't, however, consider my "schizoanalytic cartographies"[4] to be scientific theories. Just as an artist borrows from his precursors and contem-
poraries the traits which suit him, I invite those who read me to
take or reject my concepts freely. The important thing is not the

final result but the fact that the multicomponential cartographic method can co-exist with the process of subjectivation, and
that a reappropriation, an autopoiesis, of the means of production of subjectivity can be made possible.

Of course, I am not equating either psychosis to the work of
art or the psychoanalyst to the artist! I am only emphasising
that the existential registers concerned here involve a dimension of autonomy of an aesthetic order. We are faced with an
important ethical choice: either we objectify, reify, "scientifise"
subjectivity, or, on the contrary, we try to grasp it in the dimension of its processual creativity. Kant established that the
judgement of taste involved subjectivity and its relation to the
other in a certain attitude of "disinterestedness."[5] But it is not
enough to designate the categories of disinterestedness and
freedom as the essential dimension of the unconscious aesthetic
without clarifying their active mode of insertion into the psyche. How do certain semiotic segments achieve their autonomy, start to work for themselves and to secrete new fields of reference? It is from such a rupture that an existential singularisation correlative to the genesis of new coefficients of freedom will
become possible. This detachment of an ethico-aesthetic "partial object" from the field of dominant significations corresponds both to the promotion of a mutant desire and to the
achievement of a certain disinterestedness. Here I would like to
establish a bridge between the concept of a partial object (object
"a" as theorised by Lacan) that marks the autonomisation of
the components of unconscious subjectivity, and the subjective
autonomisation relative to the aesthetic object. At this point we
rediscover a problematic highlighted by Mikhaïl Bakhtin in his
first theoretical essay[6] of 1924: the function of enunciative
appropriation of aesthetic form by the autonomisation of cognitive or ethical content and the realisation of this content in an
aesthetic object — what I will call a partial enunciator. I am

attempting to draw the psychoanalytic partial object that is
adjacent to the body — the point of coupling of the drive —
towards a partial enunciation. The expansion of the notion of
partial object, to which Lacan contributed with the inclusion of
the gaze and the voice in the object "a", needs to be followed
up. This entails expanding the category to cover the full range
of nuclei of subjective autonomisation relative to group sub-
jects, and to instances of the production of subjectivity
(machinic, ecological, archictectural, religious, etc.). Bakhtin
described a transference of subjectivation operating between
the author and the contemplator of a work of art — the "spectator" in Marcel Duchamp's sense. According to Bakhtin, in
this movement the "consumer" in some way becomes co-cre-
ator; the aesthetic form only achieving this result through the
device of an isolating or separating function of such a kind that
the expressive material becomes formally creative. The content
of the work of art detaches itself from its connotations that are
as much cognitive as aesthetic: "isolation or detachment
relates not to the material, not to the work as thing, but to its
significance, to its content, which is freed from certain necessary connections with the unity of nature and the unity of the
ethical event of being."[7] There is thus a certain type of frag-
ment of content that "takes possession of the author" to engender a certain mode of aesthetic enunciation. In music, for
example, as Bakhtin emphasises, isolation and invention cannot be axiologically related to the material: "It is not the sound
of acoustics that is isolated, and not the mathematical number
of the compositional order that is made up. What is detached
and fictively irreversible is the event of striving, the axiological
tension, which actualises itself thanks to that without any
impediment, and becomes consummated."[8] In the domain of
poetry, in order to detach itself, autonomise itself, culminate
itself, creative subjectivity will tend to seize upon:

1. the sonority of the word, its musical aspect;
2. its material significations with their nuances and variants;
3. its verbal connections;
4. its emotional, intonational and volitional aspects;
5. the feeling of verbal activity in the active generation of a signifying sound, including motor elements of articulation, gesture, mime; the feeling of a movement in which the whole organism together with the activity and soul of the word are swept along in their concrete unity.

And it is this last aspect, declares Bakhtin, that encompasses all the others.[9]

These penetrating analyses can lead to an extension of our approach to partial subjectivation. Equally, we find with Bakhtin the idea of irreversibility of the aesthetic object and implicitly the idea of autopoiesis — notions truly necessary to the analysis of Unconscious formations, pedagogy, psychiatry, and more generally to a social field devastated by capitalist subjectivity. Thus it is not only in the context of music and poetry that we see the work of such fragments detached from content, fragments which I place in the category of "existential refrains." The polyphony of modes of subjectivation actually corresponds to a multiplicity of ways of "keeping time." Other rhythmics are thus led to crystallise existential assemblages, which they embody and singularise.

The simplest examples of refrains delimiting existential Territories can be found in the ethology of numerous bird species. Certain specific song sequences serve to seduce a sexual partner, warn off intruders, or announce the arrival of predators.[10] Each time this involves marking out a well-defined functional space. In archaic societies, it is through rhythms, chants, dances, masks, marks on the body, ground and totems, on ritual occasions and with mythical references, that other kinds of collective existential Territories are circumscribed.[11] One finds

these sorts of refrains in Greek Antiquity with the "nomes" that
constituted, in a way, the "signature tunes" the banners and
seals for professional associations. But we all familiar with such
crossings of subjective thresholds triggered by a catalysing temporal module that plunges us into sadness or indeed, into an
ambience of gaiety and excitement. What we are aiming at
with this concept of refrain aren't just massive affects, but
hyper-complex refrains, catalysing the emergence of incorporeal Universes such as those of music or mathematics, and crystallising the most deterritorialised existential Territories. This
type of transversalist refrain evades strict spatio-temporal
delimitation. With it, time ceases to be exterior in order to
become an intensive nucleus [foyer] of temporalisation. From
this perspective, universal time appears to be no more than a
hypothetical projection, a time of generalised equivalence, a
"flattened" capitalistic time; what is important are these partial
modules of temporalisation, operating in diverse domains (biological, ethological, socio-cultural, machinic, cosmic...), and
out of which complex refrains constitute highly relative existential synchronies.

To illustrate this mode of production of polyphonic subjectivity, where a complex refrain plays a dominant role, consider
the example of televisual consumption. When I watch television, I exist at the intersection: 1. of a perceptual fascination
provoked by the screen's luminous animation which borders
on the hypnotic,[12] 2. of a captive relation with the narrative
content of the program, associated with a lateral awareness of
surrounding events (water boiling on the stove, a child's cry,
the telephone...), 3. of a world of fantasms occupying my day-
dreams. My feeling of personal identity is thus pulled in different directions. How can I maintain a relative sense of unicity,
despite the diversity of components of subjectivation that pass
through me? It's a question of the refrain that fixes me in front

of the screen, henceforth constituted as a projective existential node. My identity has become that of the speaker, the person who speaks from the television. Like Bakhtin, I would say that the refrain is not based on elements of form, material or ordinary signification, but on the detachment of an existential "motif" (or leitmotiv) which installs itself like an "attractor" within a sensible and significational chaos. The different components conserve their heterogeneity, but are nevertheless captured by a refrain which couples them to the existential Territory of my self. In the case of neurotic identity, sometimes the refrain develops into a "hardened" representation, for example, an obsessive ritual. If for any reason this machine of subjectivation is threatened, the whole personality may implode; this occurs in pyschosis where the partial components move off on delirious, hallucinatory lines.... The paradoxical concept of a complex refrain will enable us, in psychoanalytic treatment, to refer an interpretive event, no longer to Universals or mathemes, nor to preestablished structures of subjectivity, but rather to what I call a constellation of Universes. This does not involve Universes of reference in general, but incorporeal domains of entities we detect at the same time that we produce them, and which appear to have been always there, from the moment we engender them. Here is the real paradox of these Universes: they are given in the creative moment, like a hecceity freed from discursive time — nuclei of eternity lodged between instants. What's more, over and above the elements of the situation (familial, sexual, conflictual), they involve accounting for the projection of all the lines of virtuality opening up from the event of their appearance. Take a simple example: a patient in the course of treatment remains stuck on a problem, going around in circles, and coming up against a wall. One day he says, without giving it much thought: "I've been thinking of taking up driving lessons again, I haven't dri-

ven for years"; or, "I feel like learning word processing." A
remark of this kind may remain unnoticed in a traditional conception of analysis. However, this kind of singularity can
become a key, activating a complex refrain, which will not only
modify the immediate behaviour of the patient, but open up
new fields of virtuality for him: the renewal of contact with
long lost acquaintances, revisiting old haunts, regaining self-
confidence.... In this, a rigid neutrality or non-intervention
would be negative; it's sometimes necessary to jump at the
opportunity, to approve, to run the risk of being wrong, to give
it a go, to say, "yes, perhaps this experience is important."
Respond to the event as the potential bearer of new constellations of Universes of reference. This is why I have opted for
pragmatic interventions orientated towards the construction of
subjectities, towards the production of fields of virtualities
which wouldn't simply be polarised by a symbolic hermeneutic
centered on childhood.

In this conception of analysis, time is not something to be
endured; it is activated, orientated, the object of qualitative
change. Analysis is no longer the transferential interpretation
of symptoms as a function of a preexisting, latent content, but
the invention of new catalytic nuclei capable of bifurcating
existence. A singularity, a rupture of sense, a cut, a fragmentation, the detachment of a semiotic content — in a dadaist or
surrealist manner — can originate mutant nuclei of subjectivation. Just as chemistry has to purify complex mixtures to
extract atomic and homogeneous molecular matter, thus creating an infinite scale of chemical entities that have no prior existence, the same is true in the "extraction" and "separation" of
aesthetic subjectivities or partial objects, in the psychoanalytic
sense, that make an immense complexification of subjectivity
possible — harmonies, polyphonies, counterpoints, rhythms

and existential orchestrations, until now unheard and unknown. An essentially precarious, deterritorialising complexification, constantly threatened by a reterritorialising subsidence; above all in the contemporary context where the primacy of information fluxes that are machinically engendered threaten to lead to a generalised dissolution of old existential Territorialities. In the early phases of industrial society the "demonic" still continued to flower, but since then mystery has become a rarer and rarer commodity. One need only evoke the desperate quest of Witkiewicz to grasp an ultimate "strangeness of being" which literally appeared to slip between his fingers. In these conditions, the task of the poetic function, in an enlarged sense, is to recompose artificially rarefied, resingularised Universes of subjectivation. For them, it's not a matter of transmitting messages, investing images as aids to identification, patterns of behaviour as props for modelisation procedures, but of catalysing existential operators capable of acquiring consistence and persistence.

This poetic-existential catalysis that we find at work in the midst of scriptural, vocal, musical or plastic discursivities engages quasi-synchronically the enunciative crystallisation of the creator, the interpreter and the admirer of the work of art, like analyst and patient. Its efficiency lies in its capacity to promote active, processual ruptures within semiotically structured, significational and denotative networks, where it will put emergent subjectivity to work, in Daniel Stern's sense. When it is effectively triggered in a given enunciative area — that is, situated in a historical and geo-political perspective — such an analytico-poetic function establishes itself as a mutant nuclues of auto-referentiality and auto-valorisation. This is why we must always consider it in two ways: 1. as a molecular rupture, an imperceptible bifurcation capable of overthrowing the framework of dominant redundancies, the organisation of the "already classified" or, if one prefers, the classical order. 2. in the way that it selects certain segments of these very chains of redundancy, to confer on them the a-signifying existential function I have just evoked, thereby "refraining" them and producing virulent, partial fragments of enunciation operating as "shifters" of subjectivation. The quality of the base material matters little here, as one can see in repetitive music or Butoh dance, which, as Marcel Duchamp would have wished, are turned entirely towards "the spectator." What does matter is the mutant rhythmic impetus of a temporalisation able to hold together the heterogeneous components of a new existential edifice.

Beyond the poetic function, the question of the apparatuses of subjectivation presents itself. And, more precisely, what must characterise them so that they abandon seriality — in Sartre's sense — and enter into processes of singularisation which restore to existence what we might call its auto-essentialisation. With the fading antagonisms of the Cold War, we enter a period when serious threats, posed by our productivist society to the human species, appear more distinctly. Our survival on this planet is not only threatened by environmental damage but by a degeneration in the fabric of social solidarity and in the modes of psychical life, which must literally be re-invented. The refoundation of politics will have to pass through the aesthetic and analytical dimensions implied in the three ecologies — the environment, the socius and the psyche. We cannot conceive of solutions to the poisoning of the atmosphere and to global warming due to the greenhouse effect, or to the problem of population control, without a mutation of mentality, without promoting a new art of living in society. We cannot conceive of international discipline in this domain without solving the problem of hunger and hyperinflation in the Third World. We cannot conceive of a collective recomposition of the socius, correlative to a resingularisation of subjectivity, without a new way of conceiving political and economic democracies that respect cultural differences — without multiple molecular revolutions. We cannot hope for an amelioration in the living conditions of the human species without a considerable effort to improve the feminine condition. The entire division of labour, its modes of valorisation and finalities need to be rethought. Production for the sake of production — the obsession with the rate of growth, whether in the capitalist market or in planned economies — leads to monstrous absurdities. The only acceptable finality of human activity is the production of a subjectivity that is auto-enriching its relation to the world in a continuous fashion. The productive apparatuses of subjectivity can exist at the level of megapoles as easily as at the level of an individual's language games. And to learn the intimate workings of this production, these ruptures of meaning that are auto-foundational of existence — poetry today might have more to teach us than economic science, the human sciences and psychoanalysis combined.

That contemporary social transformations happen on a large scale by a relatively progressive mutation of subjectivity, or in the moderately conservative fashion one sees in the Eastern bloc, or in the clearly reactionary, indeed neo-fascistic manner in the Middle East, and that, at the same time, such changes can take place on a molecular level, microphysical in Foucault's sense, in political activity, in analytic treatment, in establishing an apparatus changing the life of the neighbourhood, the way a school or psychiatric institution functions — the synergy of these two processes calls for a departure from structuralist reductionism and a refoundation of the problematic of subjectivity. A partial subjectivity — pre-personal, polyphonic, collective and machinic. Fundamentally, the question of enunciation gets decentered in relation to that of human individuation. Enunciation becomes correlative not only to the emergence of a logic of non-discursive intensities, but equally to a pathic incorporation-agglomeration of these vectors of partial subjectivity. Thus it involves rejecting the habitually universalising claims of psychological modelisation. The so-called scientific content of psychoanalytic or systemic theories (as well as mythological or religious modelising, or even the mythological models of systematic délire...) are essentially valuable for their existentialising function, that is, for the production of subjectivity. In these conditions, theoretical activity is reorientated towards a metamodelisation capable of taking into account the diversity of modelising systems. In particular it involves situating the concrete incidence of capitalistic subjectivity (the subjectivity of generalised equivalence) within the context of the continued development of the mass media, Collective Equipment and the information revolution — a subjectivity which seems likely to blot out, with its greyness, the faintest traces and last recesses of the planet's mysteries.

So we are proposing to decentre the question of the subject onto the question of subjectivity. Traditionally, the subject was conceived as the ultimate essence of individuation, as a pure, empty, prereflexive apprehension of the world, a nucleus of sensibility, of expressivity — the unifier of states of consciousness. With subjectivity we place the emphasis instead on the founding instance of intentionality. This involves taking the relation between subject and object by the middle and foregrounding the expressive instance (or the interpretant of the Peircean triad). Hereafter, this is where the question of Content will reside. Content participates in subjectivity by giving consistency to the ontological quality of Expression. It is in this reversibility of Content and Expression where what I call the existentialising function resides. Thus, we will start with the primacy of enunciative substance over the couplet of

Expression and Content.

I believe I've found a valid alternative to the structuralism
inspired by Saussure, one that relies on the Expression/Content
distinction formulated by Hjelmslev,[13] that is to say, based precisely on the potential reversibility of Expression and Content.
Going beyond Hjelmslev, I intend to consider a multiplicity of
expressive instances, whether they be of the order of Expression
or Content. Rather than playing on the Expression/Content
opposition which, with Hjelmslev, still repeats Saussure's signi-
fier/signified couplet, this would involve putting a multiplicity
of components of Expression, or substances of Expression in
parallel, in polyphony. There is a difficulty in that Hjelmslev
himself used the category of substance in a tripartite division
between matter, substance and form relating on one hand to
Expression and on the other to Content. With Hjelmslev, the
connection between Expression and Content is realised at the
level of the form of Expression and form of Content, which he
identified with each other. This common and commuting form
is a bit strange but it represents, in my opinion, a brilliant intuition, posing the question of the existence of a formal machine,
transversal to every modality of Expression and Content. There
is then, a bridge, a transversality between on one side the
machine of phonemic and syntagmatic discursivity of
Expression proper to language, and on the other, the division of
semantic unities of Content (for example, the way classification
of colours or animal categories is established). I call this common form a deterritorialised machine, an abstract machine.
The notion of an abstract semiotic machine isn't new: we find it
in Chomsky who postulates its existence at the root of language. But this concept, this Expression/Content opposition —
as well as the Chomskian concept of the abstract machine —
remained too bound up with language. For our part, we would

like to resituate semiology within the scope of an expanded, machinic conception which would free us from a simple linguistic opposition between Expression/Content, and allow us to integrate into enunciative assemblages an indefinite number of substances of Expression, such as biological codings or organisational forms belonging to the socius. From this perspective, the question of enunciative substance should also be outside the framework of Hjelmslev's tripartite division, matter-substance-form (form casting itself "like a net" over matter, thereby engendering the substance of Expression and Content). It would involve shattering the concept of substance in a pluralistic manner, and would promote the category of substance of Expression not only in semiology and semiotics, but in domains that are extra-linguistic, non-human, biological, technological, aesthetic, etc. The problem of the enunciative assemblage would then no longer be specific to a semiotic register but would traverse an ensemble of heterogeneous expressive materials. Thus a transversality between enunciative substances which can be, on one hand, linguistic, but on the other, of a machinic order, developing from "non-semiotically formed matter," to use another of Hjelmslev's expressions. Machinic subjectivity, the machinic assemblage of enunciation, agglomerates these different partial enunciations and installs itself, as it were, before and alongside the subject-object relation. It has, moreover, a collective character, it is multi-componential, a machinic multiplicity. Finally, it includes incorporeal dimensions, which perhaps constitutes its most problematic aspect, and one that Noam Chomsky only touches on in his attempt to make use of the Medieval concept of Universals.

Expressive, linguistic and non-linguistic substances install themselves at the junction of discursive chains (belonging to a finite, preformed world, the world of the Lacanian Other) and incorporeal registers with infinite, creationist virtualities (which have nothing to do with Lacanian "mathemes"). It is in this zone of intersection that subject and object fuse and establish their foundations. It concerns a given that phenomenologists have addressed when they demonstrate that intentionality is inseparable from its object and involves a "before" in the discursive, subject-object relation. Some psychologists have focused on the relations of empathy and transitivism in infancy and psychosis. Lacan, in his early works, when still influenced by phenomenology, evoked the importance of this type of phenomenon. Generally, one can say that psychoanalysis is born at this point of object-subject fusion that we see at work in suggestion, hypnosis and hysteria. It is an attempt at reading subjective transitivism that is at the origin of Freudian theory and practice. Moreover, anthropologists, since the era of Lévi-Bruhl, Priezluski, etc., have shown that in archaic societies, there was what they call "participation," a collective subjectivity investing a certain type of object, and putting itself in the position of an existential group nucleus. In studies on new forms of art (like Deleuze's on cinema) we will see, for example, movement-images and time-images constituting the seeds of the production of subjectivity. We are not in the presence of a passively representative image, but of a vector of subjectivation. We are actually confronted by a non-discursive, pathic knowledge, which presents itself as a subjectivity that one actively meets, an absorbant subjectivity given immediately in all its complexity. We can trace this intuition to Bergson, who shed light on the non-discursive experience of duration by opposing it to a time cut up into present, past and future, according to spatial schemas. It is true that this pathic subjectivity, before the subject-object relation, continues to self-actualise through energetico-spatio-temporal coordinates, in the world of language and through multiple mediations; but what allows us to grasp the force involved in the production of sub-

jectivity is the apprehension through it of a pseudo-discursivity,
a detournement of discursivity, which installs itself at the foundation of the subject-object relation, in a subjective pseudo-
mediation.

This pathic subjectivation, at the root of all modes of subjectivation, is overshadowed in rationalist, capitalistic subjectivity
which tends to systematically circumvent it. Science is constructed by bracketing these factors of subjectivation, which
achieve Expression only when certain discursive links are put
outside of signification. Freudianism, although impregnated
with scientism, can, in its early stages, be characterised as a
rebellion against a positivist reductionism which tended to do
without these pathic dimensions. In Freudianism the symptom,
the lapsus or joke are conceived as detached objects allowing a
mode of subjectivity, which has lost its consistency, to find the
path to a "coming into existence." The symptom through its
own repetitiveness functions like an existential refrain. The
paradox resides in the fact that pathic subjectivity tends to be
constantly evacuated from relations of discursivity, although
discursive operators are essentially based on it. The existential
function of assemblages of enunciation consists in this utilisa-
tion of links of discursivity to establish a system of repetition, of
intensive insistence, polarised between a territorialised existential Territory and deterritorialised incorporeal Universes — two
metapsychological functions we can describe as onto-genetic.
The Universes of referential value confer their own texture on
machines of Expression articulated in machinic Phylums.
Complex refrains, beyond the simple refrains of territorialisation, restates the singular consistency of these Universes. (For
example, the pathic apprehension of harmonic resonances
based on the diatonic scale deploys the "foundation" of consistency of polyphonic music, just as in another context the
apprehension of the possible concatenation of numbers and

algorithms deploys the foundation of mathematical idealities.)
The abstract machinic consistency which is thus conferred on
assemblages of enunciation resides in the layering and ordering
of partial levels of existential territorialisation. What's more,
the complex refrain functions as an interface between actualised registers of discursivity and non-discursive Universes of
virtuality. It is the most deterritorialised aspect of the refrain, its
dimension of incorporeal Universes of value which takes control of the most territorialised strata. It does this through a
movement of deterritorialisation that develops fields of the possible, tensions in value, relations of heterogeneity, of alterity, of
becoming other. The difference between these Universes of
value and Platonic Ideas is that the former do not have a fixed
character. They involve constellations of Universes, within
which a component can affirm itself over others and modify the
initial referential configuration and dominant mode of valorisation. (For example, we can see throughout the course of
Antiquity the primacy of a military machine based on metal
weapons affirming itself over the despotic State machine, the
writing machine, the religious machine, etc.) The crystallisation of such constellations can be "overtaken" during the
course of historical discursivity, but never wiped out since it is
an irreversible rupture in the incorporeal memory of collective
subjectivity. Thus we are situated totally outside the vision of a
Being moving unchanged through the universal history of
ontological formations. There are singular incorporeal constellations which belong to natural and human history and at the
same time escape them by a thousand lines of flight. The
moment mathematical Universes started to appear, it is no
longer possible to act as though the abstract machines which
support them had not always existed everywhere and for all
time and as though they do not project themselves onto future
possibles. We can no longer act as though polyphonic music

had not been invented for the rest of time, both past and future. Such is the first stratum of ontological consistency of this function of existential subjectivation, which is situated within the perspective of a certain axiological creationism.

The second is the embodiment of these values in the irreversibility of the being-there of existential Territories, which confer their character of autopoiesis and singularity on to the zones of subjectivation. In the logic of discursive ensembles which dictates the domains of Fluxes and machinic Phylums, there is always a separation between the poles of subject and object. The truth of a proposition answers to the law of the excluded middle; each object appears in a relationship of binary opposition with a "foundation." Whereas in pathic logic, there is no extrinsic global reference that can be circumscribed. The object relation is destabilised, and the functions of subjectivation are put into question. An incorporeal universe is not supported by coordinates embedded in the world, but by ordinates, by an intensive ordination coupled for better or worse to these existential Territories. Territories which claim to encompass, in a single movement, the sum of everyday existence but which are in fact only based on derisory refrains, indexing if not their vacuity then at least the degree zero of their ontological intensity: thus Territories never given as object but always as intensive repetition, as piercing existential affirmation. And I repeat, this operation is effected through the borrowing of semiotic links, detached and diverted from their signifying and coding tasks. Here, an expressive instance is based on a matter-form relation, which extracts complex forms from a chaotic material.

The logic of discursive sets finds a kind of desperate fulfilment in Capital, the Signifier, and Being with a capital B. Capital is the referent for the generalised equivalence between labour and goods; the Signifier the capitalistic referent for semiological expression, the great reducer of ontological polyvocality. The true, the good, the beautiful are "normalising" categories for processes which escape the logic of circumscribed sets. They are empty referents, they create a void, they install transcendence in the relations of representation. To choose Capital, the Signifier or Being, is to participate in a similar ethicopolitical option. Capital smashes all other modes of valorisation. The Signifier silences the infinite virtualities of minor languages and partial expressions. Being is like an imprisonment which blinds us to the richness and multivalence of Universes of value which, nevertheless, proliferate under our noses. There is an ethical choice in favour of the richness of the possible, an ethics and politics of the virtual that decorporealises and deterritorialises contingency, linear causality and the pressure of circumstances and significations which besiege us. It is a choice for processuality, irreversibility and resingularisation. On a small scale, this redeployment can turn itself into the mode of entrapment, of impoverishment, indeed of catastrophe in neurosis. It can take up reactive religious references. It can annihilate itself in alcohol, drugs, television, an endless daily grind. But it can also make use of other procedures that are more collective, more social, more political ...

In order to question dualist oppositions, such as Being-being or Subject-Object, and systems of Manichean bipolar valorisations, I have proposed the concept of ontological intensity. It implies an ethico-aesthetic engagement with the enunciative assemblage, both in actual and virtual registers. But another element of the metamodelisation proposed here resides in the collective character of machinic multiplicities. There is no personological totalisation of the different components of Expression, or the self-enclosed totalisation of Universes of reference, either in the sciences, the arts or in society. There is an

agglomeration of heterogeneous factors of subjectivation.
Machinic segments refer to a detotalised, deterritorialised
mecanosphere, to an infinite play of interface. There is no Being
already installed throughout temporality. This questioning of
dual, binary relations (Being-being, or Conscious-Unconscious)
implies a questioning of semiotic linearity — which always
seems to be beyond question. Pathic expression is not placed in a
relation of discursive succession in order to situate the object on
the basis of a clearly delimited referent. Here we are in a register
of co-existence, of crystallisation of intensity. Time does not exist
as an empty container (a conception which remains at the root
of Einsteinian thought). The relations of temporalisation are
essentially those of machinic synchrony. There is a deployment
of axiological ordinates, without the constitution of a referent
exterior to this deployment. Here we are before the relation of
"extensionalising" linearity, between an object and its representative mediation within an abstract machinic complexion.

Will we say of the incorporeal and virtual part of assemblages of enunciation that it is *in voce* according to a "termin-
ist," nominalist viewpoint, which makes semiotic entities the
tributaries of a pure subjectivity; or will we say that they are *in
re* within the framework of a realist conception of the world,
subjectivity being only an illusory artefact? But maybe it's necessary to affirm both these positions concurrently: the domain
of virtual intensities establishing itself prior to distinctions
being made between the semiotic machine, the referred object
and the enunciative subject. It's from a failure to see that
machinic segments are autopoietic and ontogenetic that one
endlessly makes universalist reductions to the Signifier and to
scientific rationality. Machinic interfaces are heterogenetic;
they summon the alterity of the points of view we might have
on them and, as a consequence, on the systems of metamodelisation which allow us to account, in one way or another, for the

fundamentally inaccessible character of their autopoietic nuclei. We need to free ourselves from a solitary reference to technological machines and expand the concept of machine so as to situate the machine's adjacence to incorporeal Universes of reference. Note that the categories of metamodelisation proposed here — Fluxes, machinic Phylums, existential Territories, incorporeal Universes — are only of interest because they come in fours and allow us to break free of tertiary descriptions which always end up falling back into dualisms. The fourth term stands for an nth term: it is the opening onto multiplicity. What distinguishes metamodelisation from modelisation is the way it uses terms to develop possible openings onto the virtual and onto creative processuality.

1   Daniel Stern, *The Interpersonal World of the Infant*, Basic Books, New York, 1985. See later pp.65-6.

2   Francisco Varela, *Autonomie et Connaissance*, Le Seuil, Paris, 1989. [This is a revised French edition of *Principles of Biological Autonomy*, North Holland Press, New York, 1979.]

3   Mony Elkaim, *If You Love Me, Don't Love Me*, Basic Books, New York, 1990.

4   Félix Guattari, *Cartographies schizoanalytiques*, Galilée, Paris, 1989.

5   "Of all these three kinds of delight (in the agreeable, the beautiful, and the good), that of taste in the beautiful may be said to be the one and only disinterested and free delight; for, with it, no interest, whether of sense or reason extorts approval." Immanuel Kant, *The Critique of Judgement*, trans. James Creed Meredith, Clarendon Press, Oxford, 1982, p.49.

6   Mikhaïl Bakhtin,"Content, Material, and Form in Verbal Art," in *Art and Answerability: Eary Philosophical Essays by M.M.Baktin*, edited by Michael Hoquist and Vadim Liapunov, University of Texas Press, Austin, 1990.

7   Ibid., p.306.

8   Ibid., p.307.

9   Ibid., p.307.

10 Félix Guattari, *L'Inconscient machinique*, Recherche, Paris, 1979.
11 See the role of dreams in the mythical cartographies of Australian Aborigines. Barbara Glocewski, *Les Rêveurs du désert*, Plon, Paris, 1989.
12 For a re-examination of hypnosis and suggestion, see Léon Chertok and Isabelle Stengers, *A Critique of Psychoanalytic Reason: Hypnosis as a Scientific Problem from Lavoisier to Lacan*, trans. Martha N Evans, Stanford University Press, Stanford, 1992.
13 Louis Hjelmslev, *Prolegomena to a Theory of Language*, trans. Francis J. Whitfield, University of Wisconsin Press, Madison, 1969); *Language: an introduction*, Wisconsin University Press, Madison, 1970; *Essais linguistiques*, Minuit, Paris, 1971; *Nouveaux Essais*, PUF, Paris, 1985.

2

Machinic heterogenesis

Common usage suggests that we speak of the machine as a subset of technology. We should, however, consider the problematic of technology as dependent on machines, and not the inverse. The machine would become the prerequisite for technology rather than its expression. Machinism is an object of fascination, sometimes of délire, about which there's a whole historical "bestiary." Since the origin of philosophy, the relationship between man and machine has been the object of interrogation. Aristotle thought that the goal of techne was to create what nature found impossible to accomplish. Being of the order of "knowledge" and not of "doing," techne interposes a kind of creative mediation between nature and humanity whose status of intercession is a source of perpetual ambiguity. "Mechanist" conceptions of the machine empty it of everything that would enable it to avoid a simple construction *partes extra partes*. "Vitalist" conceptions assimilate the machine to living beings; unless it is living beings that are assimilated to machines. The "cybernetic" perspective developed by Norbert Wiener[1] envisages living systems as particular types of machines equipped with the principle of feedback. More recent "systemic" conceptions (Humberto Maturana and Francisco Varela) develop the concept of autopoiesis (auto-production), reserving it for living machines. Following Heidegger, a philosophical fashion entrusts techne — in its opposition to modern technology — with the mission of "unmasking the truth" that "seeks the true in the exact." Thus it nails techne to an ontological plinth — to a *grund* — and compromises its character of processual opening.

Through these positions, we will attempt to discern various levels of ontological intensity and envisage machinism in its totality, in its technological, social, semiotic and axiological avatars. And this will involve a reconstruction of the concept of machine that goes far beyond the technical machine. For each type of machine, we will pose a question, not about its vital autonomy — it's not an animal — but about its singular power of enunciation: what I call its specific enunciative consistency. The first type of machine we are going to consider is the material apparatus. They are made by the hand of man — itself taken over by other machines — according to conceptions and plans which respond to the goals of production. These different stages I will call ˄ finalised, diagrammatic schemas. But already this montage and these finalisations impose the necessity of expanding the limits of the machine, *stricto sensu*, to the functional ensemble which associates it with man. We will see that this implies taking into account multiple components:
— material and energy components
— semiotic, diagrammatic and algorithmic components (plans, formulae, equations and calculations which lead to the fabrication of the machine);
components of organs, influx and humours of the human body;
— individual and collective mental representations and information;
— investments of desiring machines producing a subjectivity adjacent to these components;

— abstract machines installing themselves transversally to the machinic levels previously considered (material, cognitive, affective and social).

When we speak of abstract machines, by "abstract" we can also understand "extract" in the sense of extracting. They are montages capable of relating all the heterogeneous levels that they traverse and that we have just enumerated. The abstract machine is transversal to them, and it is this abstract machine that will or will not give these levels an existence, an efficiency, a power of ontological auto-affirmation. The different components are swept up and reshaped by a sort of dynamism. Such a functional ensemble will hereafter be described as a machinic assemblage. The term assemblage does not imply any notion of bond, passage, or anastomosis between its components. It is an assemblage of possible fields, of virtual as much as constituted elements, without any notion of generic or species' relation. In this context, utensils, instruments, the most basic tools and the least structured pieces of a machine acquire the status of a proto-machine.

Let us take an example. If we take a hammer apart by removing its handle, it is still a hammer but in a "mutilated" state. The "head" of the hammer — another zoomorphic metaphor — can be reduced by fusion. It will then cross a threshold of formal consistency where it will lose its form; this machinic gestalt works moreover as much on a technological plane as on an imaginary level, to evoke the dated memory of the hammer and sickle. We are simply in the presence of metallic mass returned to smoothness, to the deterritorialisation which precedes its appearance in a machinic form. To go beyond this type of experiment — comparable to the piece of Cartesian wax — let us attempt the inverse, to associate the hammer with the arm, the nail with the anvil. Between them they maintain relations of syntagmatic linkage. And their "collective dance"

can bring to life the defunct guild of blacksmiths, the sinister
epoch of ancient iron mines, the ancestral use of metal-rimmed
wheels ... Leroi-Gourhan emphasised that the technical object
was nothing outside of the technical ensemble to which it
belonged. It is the same for sophisticated machines such as
robots, which will soon be engendered by other robots. Human
action remains adjacent to their gestation, waiting for the
breakdown which will require its intervention: this residue of a
direct act. But doesn't all this suggest a partial view, a certain
taste for a dated period of science fiction? Curiously, in acquiring more and more life, machines demand in return more and
more abstract human vitality: and this has occurred throughout their evolutionary development. Computers, expert systems
and artificial intelligence add as much to thought as they sub-
tract from thinking. They relieve thought of inert schemas. The
forms of thought assisted by computer are mutant, relating to
other musics, other Universes of reference.[2]

It is, then, impossible to deny the participation of human
thought in the essence of machinism. But up to what point can
this thought still be described as human? Doesn't technico-scientific thought fall within the province of a certain type of mental and semiotic machinism? What we need here is a distinction
between on the one hand semiologies that produce significations, the common currency of social groups — like the
"human" enunciation of people who work with machines —
and on the other, a-signifying semiotics which, regardless of
the quantity of significations they convey, handle figures of
expression that might be qualified as "non-human" (such as
equations and plans which enunciate the machine and make it
act in a diagrammatic capacity on technical and experimental
apparatuses). The semiologies of signification play in keys with
distinctive oppositions of a phonematic or scriptural order
which transcribe enunciations into materials of signifying

expression. Structuralists have been content to erect the Signifier as a category unifying all expressive economies: language, the icon, gesture, urbanism or the cinema, etc. They have postulated a general signifying translatability for all forms of discursivity. But in so doing, have they not misunderstood the essential dimension of machinic autopoiesis? This continual emergence of sense and effects does not concern the redundancy of mimesis but rather the production of an effect of singular sense, even though indefinitely reproducible.

This autopoietic node in the machine is what separates and differentiates it from structure and gives it value. Structure implies feedback loops, it puts into play a concept of totalisation that it itself masters. It is occupied by inputs and outputs whose purpose is to make the structure function according to a principle of eternal return. It is haunted by a desire for eternity. The machine, on the contrary, is shaped by a desire for abolition. Its emergence is doubled with breakdown, catastrophe — the menace of death. It possesses a supplement: a dimension of alterity which it develops in different forms. This alterity differentiates it from structure, which is based on a principle of homeomorphism. The difference supplied by machinic autopoiesis is based on disequilibrium, the prospection of virtual Universes far from equilibrium. And this doesn't simply involve a rupture of formal equilibrium, but a radical ontological reconversion. The machine always depends on exterior elements in order to be able to exist as such. It implies a complementarity, not just with the man who fabricates it, makes it function or destroys it, but it is itself in a relation of alterity with other virtual or actual machines — a "non-human" enunciation, a proto-subjective diagram.

This ontological reconversion dismisses the totalising scope of the concept of the Signifier. Because the signifying entities

which operate the diverse mutations of the ontological referent
— that makes us move from the Universe of molecular chemistry to the Universe of biological chemistry, or from the
acoustic world to the world of polyphonic and harmonic music
— are not the same. Of course, lines of signifying decoding,
composed of discrete figures — binarisable, syntagmatisable
and paradigmatisable — sometimes appear in one Universe or
another. And we can have the illusion that the same signifying
network occupies all these domains. It is, however, totally different when we consider the actual texture of these Universes
of reference. They are always stamped with the mark of singularity. From acoustics to polyphonic music, there is a diver-
gence of constellations of expressive intensity. They involve a
certain pathic relationship, and convey irreducibly heterogeneous ontological consistencies. We thus discover as many
types of deterritorialisation as traits of expressive materials. The
signifying articulation hanging over them — in its indifferent
neutrality — is incapable of imposing itself as a relation of
immanence to machinic intensities, to this non-discursive,
auto-enunciating, auto-valorising, autopoietic node. It does
not submit to any general syntax of the procedures of deterritorialisation. No couplet — Being-being, Being-Nothingness,
being-other — can claim the status of an ontological binary
digit. Machinic propositions elude the ordinary games of discursivity and the structural coordinates of energy, time and
space.

Yet an ontological transversality does nonetheless exist in
them. What happens at a level of the particulate-cosmic is not
without relation to the human soul or events in the socius. But
not according to harmonic universals of the Platonic
type (*Sophist*). The composition of deterritorialising intensities
is incarnated in abstract machines. We should bear in mind
that there is a machinic essence which will incarnate itself in a

technical machine, and equally in the social and cognitive environment connected to this machine — social groups are also machines, the body is a machine, there are scientific, theoretical and information machines. The abstract machine passes through all these heterogeneous components but above all it heterogenises them, beyond any unifying trait and according to a principle of irreversibility, singularity and necessity. In this respect the Lacanian signifier is struck with a double lack: it is too abstract in that it makes heterogeneous, expressive materials translatable, it lacks ontological heterogenesis, it gratuitously uniformises and syntaxises diverse regions of being, and, at the same time, it is not abstract enough because it is incapable of taking into account the specificity of these machinic autopoietic nodes, to which we must now return.

Francisco Varela characterises a machine by "the set of inter-relations of its components independent of the components themselves."[3] The organisation of a machine thus has no connection with its materiality. He distinguishes two types of machines: "allopoietic" machines which produce something other than themselves, and "autopoietic" machines which engender and specify their own organisation and limits. Autopoietic machines undertake an incessant process of the replacement of their components as they must continually compensate for the external perturbations to which they are exposed. In fact, the qualification of autopoietic is reserved by Varela for the biological domain: social systems, technical machines, crystalline systems, etc., are excluded. This is the sense of his distinction between allopoiesis and autopoiesis. But autopoiesis, which uniquely defines autonomous entities — unitary, individuated and closed to input/output relationships — lacks characteristics essential to living organisms, like the fact that they are born, die and survive through genetic phylums. Autopoiesis deserves to be rethought in terms of evolutionary, collective entities, which maintain diverse types of relations of alterity, rather than being implacably closed in on themselves. In such a case, institutions and technical machines appear to be allopoietic, but when one considers them in the context of the machinic assemblages they constitute with human beings, they become ipso facto autopoietic. Thus we will view autopoiesis from the perspective of the ontogenesis and phlyogenesis proper to a mecanosphere superposed on the biosphere.

The phylogenetic evolution of machinism is expressed, at a primary level, by the fact that machines appear across "generations," one suppressing the other as it becomes obsolete. The filiation of previous generations is prolonged into the future by lines of virtuality and their arborent implications. But this is not a question of a univocal historical causality. Evolutionary lines appear in rhizomes; datings are not synchronic but heterochronic. Example: the industrial "take off" of steam engines happened centuries after the Chinese Empire had used them as children's toys. In fact, these evolutionary rhizomes move in blocks across technical civilisations. A technological innovation may know long periods of stagnation or regression, but there are few cases in which it does not "restart" at a later date. This is particularly clear with military technological innovations: they frequently punctuate long historical periods that they stamp with the seal of irreversibility, wiping out empires for the benefit of new geopolitical configurations. But, and I repeat it, this was already true of the most humble instruments, utensils and tools which don't escape this phylogenesis. One could, for example, dedicate an exhibition to the evolution of the hammer since the Iron Age and conjecture about what it will become in the context of new materials and technologies. The hammer that one buys today at the supermarket is, in a way, "drawn out" on a phylogenetic line of infinite, virtual extension.

It is at the intersection of heterogeneous machinic Universes, of different dimensions and with unfamiliar ontological textures, radical innovations and once forgotten, then reactivated, ancestral machinic lines, that the movement of history singularises itself. Among other components, the Neolithic machine associates the machine of spoken language, machines of hewn stone, agrarian machines based on the selection of grains and a village proto-economy. The writing machine will only emerge with the birth of urban megamachines (Lewis Mumford) correlative to the spread of archaic empires. Parallel to this, the great nomadic machines constituted themselves out of the collusion between the metallurgic machine and new war machines. As for the great capitalistic machines, their foundational machinisms were prolific: urban State machines, then royal machines, commercial and banking machines, navigation machines, monotheist religious machines, deterritorialised musical and plastic machines, scientific and technical machines, etc.

The question of the reproducibility of the machine on an ontogenetic level is more complex. Maintaining a machine's operationality — its functional identity — is never absolutely guaranteed: wear and tear, fine balance, breakdowns and entropy demand a renewal of its material components, its energy and information components, the latter able to be lost in "noise." Equally, the maintenance of a machinic assemblage's consistency demands that the element of human action and intelligence involved in its composition must also be renewed. The man-machine alterity is thus inextricably linked to a machine-machine alterity which operates in relations of complementarity or agonistic relations (between war machines) or again in the relations of parts or apparatuses. In fact, the wear and tear, accident, death and resurrection of a machine in a new copy or model are part of its destiny and can become central to its essence in certain aesthetic machines (the "compressions" of César, the "metamechanics," the happening machines, the delirious machines of Jean Tinguely). The reproducibility of the machine is not a pure programmed repetition. The scansions of rupture and indifferentiation, which uncouple a model from any support, introduce their own share of both ontogenetic and phylogenetic difference. It is in this phase of passage to a diagrammatic state, a disincarnate abstract machine, that the "supplements of the soul" of the machinic node are distinguished from simple material agglomerates. A heap of stones is not a machine, whereas a wall is already a static proto-machine, manifesting virtual polarities, an inside and outside, an above and below, a right and left ... These diagrammatic virtualities take us beyond Varela's characterisation of machinic autopoiesis as unitary individuation, with neither input nor output; they direct us towards a more collective machinism without delimited unity, whose autonomy accommodates diverse mediums of alterity. The reproducibility of the technical machine differs from that of living beings, in that it is not based on sequential codes perfectly circumscribed in a territorialised genome. Obviously every technological machine has its own plans for conception and assembly. But while these plans keep their distance from the machine, they also move from one machine to another so as to constitute a diagrammatic rhizome which tends to cover the mecanosphere globally. The relations of technological machines between themselves, and the way their respective parts fit together, presuppose a formal serialisation and a certain perdition of their singularity — stronger than that of living machines — correlative to a distance between the machine manifested in energetico-spatio-temporal coordinates and the diagrammatic machine which develops in more deterritorialised coordinates.

This deterritorialising distance and loss of singularity needs to be related to a reciprocal smoothing of the materials constitutive of the technical machine. Of course, singular rough patches belonging to these materials can never be completely abolished but they must only interfere with the machine's "play" if they are required to do so by its diagrammatic functioning. Let us examine these two aspects of machinic separation and smoothing, taking an apparently simple machinic apparatus — the couple formed by a lock and its key. Two types of form, with ontologically heterogeneous textures are at work here: 1) materialised, contingent, concrete and discrete forms, whose singularity is closed in on itself, embodied respectively in the profile Fl of the lock and by the profile Fk of the key. Fl and Fk never quite coincide. They evolve through time, due to wear and oxidation, but both forms must stay within the framework of a separation-type limit beyond which the key would cease to be operational; 2) "formal," diagrammatic forms, subsumed within this separation-type, which appear as a continuum including the whole range of profiles Fl, Fk, compatible with the effective operation of the lock.

One quickly notices that the machinic effect, the passage to the possible act, is entirely concerned with the second type of form. Although ranged across the most restrained separation-type limit possible, these diagrammatic forms appear infinite in number. In fact, it is a matter of an integral of forms Fk, Fl.

This infinite integral form doubles and smooths the contingent forms Fl and Fk which only have value machinically inasmuch as they belong to it. A bridge is thus established "above" the concrete, authorised forms. I call this operation deterritorialised smoothing and it applies as much to the normalisation of the machine's constitutive materials as it does to their "digital" and functional description. Ferric ore which has been insufficiently worked, or deterritorialised, retains irregularities from the milling of the original material, which would distort the ideal profiles of the lock and key. The smoothing of the material has to remove excessive aspects of contingence from it, and make it behave in a way that accurately moulds the formal imprints extrinsic to it. We should add that this moulding — in a way comparable to photography — should not be too evanescent and should conserve a properly sufficient consistency. Here again we find a separation-type phenomenon, putting into play a theoretical diagrammatic consistency. A lead or golden key risks bending in a steel lock. A key that is changed into a liquid or gaseous state immediately loses its pragmatic efficiency and departs from the field of the technical machine.

This phenomenon of a formal threshold can be found at all levels of intra- or inter-machine relations, and in particular with the existence of spare parts. The components of the technical machine are thus like the units of a currency, and this has become more evident since computers started to be used in their conception and design. These machinic forms, these smoothings of material, of a separation-type limit between parts and their functional adjustments, would suggest that form takes precedence over consistency and over material singularities — the technological machine's reproducibility appearing to dictate that each of its elements fit into a pre-established definition of a diagrammatic order. Charles Sanders Peirce, who described the diagram as an "icon of relation" and assimilated it to the function of algorithms, proposed a broader vision that is worth developing further in the present perspective. Here, the diagram is conceived as an autopoietic machine which not only gives it a functional and material consistency, but requires it to deploy its diverse registers of alterity, freeing it from an identity locked into simple structural relations. The machine's proto-subjectivity installs itself in Universes of virtuality which extend far beyond its existential territoriality. Thus

we refuse to postulate a formal subjectivity intrinsic to diagrammatic semiotisation, for example, a subjectivity "lodged"
in signifying chains according to the well-known Lacanian
principle: "a signifier represents the subject for another signifier." For the machine's diverse registers, there is no univocal
subjectivity based on cut, lack or suture, but there are ontologically heterogeneous modes of subjectivity, constellations of
incorporeal Universes of reference which take the position of
partial enunciators in multiple domains of alterity, or more precisely, domains of alterification.

We have already encountered a certain number of these
registers of machinic alterity:
— the alterity of proximity between different machines and
between different parts of the same machine;
— the alterity of an internal, material consistency;
— the alterity of formal, diagrammatic consistency;
— the alterity of the evolutionary phylum;
— the agonistic alterity between machines of war, whose pro-
longation we could associate with the "auto-agonistic" alterity
of desiring machines which tend towards their own collapsus
and abolition.

Another form of alterity which has only been approached
very indirectly, is the alterity of scale, or fractal alterity, which
establishes a play of systematic correspondences between
machines at different levels.[4] We are not, however, in the
process of drawing up a universal table of forms of machinic
alterity because, in truth, their ontological modalities are infinite.
They organise themselves into constellations of incorporeal
Universes of reference with unlimited combinatories and creativity.

Archaic societies are better equipped than White, male, capitalistic subjectivities to produce a cartography of this multivalence of alterity. With regard to this, we could refer to Marc

Augé's account of the heterogeneous registers relating to the
fetish object Legba in African societies of the Fon. The Legba
comes to being transversally in:
— a dimension of destiny;
— a universe of vital principle;
— an ancestral filiation;
— a materialised god;
— a sign of appropriation;
— an entity of individuation;
— a fetish at the entrance to the village, another at the portal of
the house and, after initiation, at the entrance to the bedroom...

The Legba is a handful of sand, a receptacle, but it's also the
expression of a relation to others. One finds it at the door, at the
market, in the village square, at crossroads. It can transmit
messages, questions, answers. It is also a way of relating to the
dead and to ancestors. It is both an individual and a class of
individuals; a name and a noun. "Its existence corresponds to
the obvious fact that the social is not simply of a relational
order but of the order of being."[5] Marc Augé stresses the impossible transparency and translatability of symbolic systems.
"The Legba apparatus [...] is constructed on two axes. One is
viewed from the exterior to the interior, the other from identity
to alterity. Thus being, identity and the relation to the other are
constructed, through fetishistic practice, not only on a symbolic basis but also in an openly ontological way."[6]

Contemporary machinic assemblages have even less standard univocal referent than the subjectivity of archaic societies.
But we are far less accustomed to the irreducible heterogeneity,
or even the heterogenetic character, of their referential components. Capital, Energy, Information, the Signifier are so many
categories which would have us believe in the ontological
homogeneity of referents (biological, ethological, economic,
phonological, scriptural, musical, etc.)

In the context of a reductionist modernity, it is up to us to rediscover that for every promotion of a machinic intersection there corresponds a specific constellation of Universes of value from the moment a partial non-human enunciation has been instituted. Biological machines promote living Universes which differentiate themselves into vegetable becomings, animal becomings. Musical machines establish themselves against a background of sonorous Universes which have been constantly modified since the great polyphonic mutation. Technical machines install themselves at the intersection of the most complex and heterogeneous enunciative components. Heidegger, who turned the world of technology into a kind of malefic destiny resulting from a movement of distancing from being, used the example of a commercial plane on a runway: the visible object conceals "what and how it is." It unveils itself "only as standing-reserve inasmuch as it is ordered to insure the possibility of transportation" and to this end, "it must be in its whole structure and in every one of its constituent parts on call for duty, i.e., ready for take-off".[7] This interpellation, this "ordering" which reveals the real as "standing-reserve" is essentially operated by man and understood in terms of a universal operation, travelling, flying ... But does this "standing-reserve" of the machine really reside in an already-there, in terms of eternal truths, revealed to the being of man? In fact the machine speaks to the machine before speaking to man and the ontological domains that it reveals and secretes are, on each occasion, singular and precarious.

Let us reconsider the example of a commercial plane, this time not generically but using the technologically dated model baptised as the Concorde. The ontological consistency of this object is essentially composite; it is at the intersection, at the point of constellation and pathic agglomeration of Universes each of which have their own ontological consistency, traits of intensity, their ordinates and coordinates, their specific machinisms. Concorde simultaneously involves:

— a diagrammatic Universe with plans of theoretical "feasibility";
— technological Universes transposing this "feasibility" into material terms;
— industrial Universes capable of effectively producing it;
— collective imaginary Universes corresponding to a desire sufficient to make it see the light of day;
— political and economic Universes leading, amongst other things, to the release of credit for its construction ...

But the bottom line is that the ensemble of these final, material, formal and efficient causes will not do the job! The Concorde object moves effectively between Paris and New York but remains nailed to the economic ground. This lack of consistency of one of its components has decisively fragilised its global ontological consistency. Concorde only exists within the limited reproducibility of twelve examples and at the root of a possibilist phylum of future supersonics. And this is hardly negligible!

Why are we so insistent about the impossibility of establishing the general translatability of diverse referential and partial enunciative components of assemblage? Why this lack of reverence towards the Lacanian conception of the signifier? Precisely because this theorising which stems from structural linguistics forbids us from entering the real world of the machine. The structuralist signifier is always synonymous with linear discursivity. From one symbol to another, the subjective effect happens without any other ontological guarantee. As opposed to this, heterogeneous machines, as envisaged from our schizonanalytical perspective, do not produce a standard being at the mercy of a universal temporalisation. To clarify this point we should establish some distinctions between the different forms of semiological, semiotic and coded linearity:

— the codings of the "natural" world, which operate on several

spatial dimensions (for example those of crystallography) and
which do not imply the extraction of autonomised operators of
coding;
— the relative linearity of biological codings, for example, the
double helix of DNA which, starting from four basic chemical
radicals, develops equally in three dimensions;
— the linearity of pre-signifying semiologies, which develop on
relatively autonomous, parallel lines, even if the phonological
chains of spoken language appear to always overcode all the
others;
— the semiological linearity of the structural signifier which
imposes itself despotically over all the other modes of semiotisation, expropriates them and even tends to make them disappear
within the framework of a communicational economy dominated by informatics (please note: informatics in its current
state, since this state of things is in no way definitive);
— the superlinearity of a-signifying substances of expression,
where the signifier loses its despotism. The informational lines
of hypertexts can recover a certain dynamic polymorphism and
work in direct contact with referent Universes which are in no
way linear and, what is more, tend to escape a logic of spa-
tialised sets.

The indicative matter of a-signifying semiotic machines is constituted by "point-signs"; these on one hand belong to a semiotic order and on the other intervene directly in a series of
material machinic processes. Example: a credit card number
which triggers the operation of a bank auto-teller. The a-signifying semiotic figures don't simply secrete significations. They
give out stop and start orders but above all activate the "bringing into being" of ontological Universes. Consider for a moment
the example of the pentatonic musical refrain which, with only
a few notes, catalyses the Debussyst constellation of multiple

Universes:

— the Wagnerian Universe surrounding Parsifal, which
attaches itself to the existential Territory constituted by
Bayreuth;

— the Universe of Gregorian chant;

— that of French music, with the return to favour of Rameau
and Couperin;

— that of Chopin, due to a nationalist transposition (Ravel, for
his part, appropriating Liszt);

— the Javanese music Debussy discovered at the Universal
Exposition of 1889;

— the world of Manet and Mallarmé, which is associated with
Debussy's stay at the Villa Médicis.

It would be appropriate to add to these past and present
influences the prospective resonances which constituted the
reinvention of polyphony from the time of the Ars Nova, its
repercussions on the French musical phylum of Ravel, Duparc,
Messiaen, etc., and on the sonorous mutation triggered by
Stravinsky, his presence in the work of Proust...

We can clearly see that there is no bi-univocal correspon-
dence between linear signifying links or archi-writing, depending on the author, and this multireferential, multidimensional
machinic catalysis. The symmetry of scale, the transversality,
the pathic non-discursive character of their expansion: all these
dimensions remove us from the logic of the excluded middle
and reinforce us in our dismissal of the ontological binarism we
criticised previously. A machinic assemblage, through its
diverse components, extracts its consistency by crossing ontological thresholds, non-linear thresholds of irreversibility, ontological and phylogenetic thresholds, creative thresholds of heterogenesis and autopoiesis. The notion of scale needs to be
expanded to consider fractal symmetries in ontological terms.
What fractal machines traverse are substantial scales. They

traverse them in engendering them. But, and this should be noted, the existential ordinates that they "invent" were always already there. How can this paradox be sustained? It's because everything becomes possible (including the recessive smoothing of time, evoked by René Thom) the moment one allows the assemblage to escape from energetico-spatio-temporal coordinates. And, here again, we need to rediscover a manner of being of Being — before, after, here and everywhere else — without being, however, identical to itself; a processual, polyphonic Being singularisable by infinitely complexifiable textures, according to the infinite speeds which animate its virtual compositions.

The ontological relativity advocated here is inseparable from an enunciative relativity. Knowledge of a Universe (in an astrophysical or axiological sense) is only possible through the mediation of autopoietic machines. A zone of self-belonging needs to exist somewhere for the coming into cognitive existence of any being or any modality of being. Outside of this machine/Universe coupling, beings only have the pure status of a virtual entity. And it is the same for their enunciative coordinates. The biosphere and mecanosphere, coupled on this planet, focus a point of view of space, time and energy. They trace an angle of the constitution of our galaxy. Outside of this particularised point of view, the rest of the Universe exists (in the sense that we understand existence here-below) only through the virtual existence of other autopoietic machines at the heart of other bio-mecanospheres scattered throughout the cosmos. The relativity of points of view of space, time and energy do not, for all that, absorb the real into the dream. The category of Time dissolves in cosmological reflections on the Big Bang even as the category of irreversibility is affirmed. Residual objectivity is what resists scanning by the infinite variation of

points of view constitutable upon it. Imagine an autopoietic
entity whose particles are constructed from galaxies. Or, con-
versely, a cognitivity constituted on the scale of quarks. A different panorama, another ontological consistency. The
mecanosphere draws out and actualises configurations which
exist amongst an infinity of others in fields of virtuality.
Existential machines are at the same level as being in its intrinsic multiplicity. They are not mediated by transcendent signifiers and subsumed by a univocal ontological foundation. They
are to themselves their own material of semiotic expression.
Existence, as a process of deterritorialisation, is a specific inter-
machinic operation which superimposes itself on the promotion of singularised existential intensities. And, I repeat, there is
no generalised syntax for these deterritorialisations. Existence
is not dialectical, not representable. It is hardly livable!

Desiring machines which break with the great interpersonal
and social organic equilibria, which invert orders, play the role
of the other as against a politics of auto-centering on the self.
For example, the partial drives and perverse polymorphic
investments of psychoanlysis don't constitute an exceptional
and deviant race of machines. All machinic assemblages har-
bour — even if in an embryonic state — enunciative zones
which are so many desiring proto-machines. To clarify this
point we need to extend our transmachinic bridge and understand the smoothing of the ontological texture of machinic
material and diagrammatic feedbacks as so many dimensions
of intensification that take us beyond the linear causalities of
the capitalistic apprehension of machinic Universes. We also
need to abandon logics based on the principles of the excluded
middle and sufficient reason. Through this smoothing there
appears a being beyond, a being-for-the-other which gives consistency to an existent beyond its strict delimitation, here and

now. The machine is always synonymous with a nucleus constitutive of an existential Territory against a background of a
constellation of incorporeal Universes of reference (or value).
The "mechanism" of this turning around of being consists in
the fact that some of the machine's discursive segments do not
only play a functional or signifying role, but assume the existentialising function of pure intensive repetition that I have
called the refrain function. The smoothing is like an ontological
refrain, and thus, far from apprehending a univocal truth of
being through techne — as Heideggerian ontology would have
it — it is a plurality of beings as machines which give themselves to us the moment we acquire the pathic and cartographic means of reaching them. The manifestations — not of Being,
but of multitudes of ontological components — are of the order
of the machine. And this, without semiological mediation,
without transcendent coding, directly as "being's giving of
itself," as giving. Acceding to such a "giving" is already to participate ontologically in it as a full right. The term right does
not occur here by chance, since at this proto-ontological level it
is already necessary to affirm a proto-ethical dimension. The
play of intensity of the ontological constellation is, in a way, a
choice of being not only for self, but for the whole alterity of the
cosmos and for the infinity of times.

If there's choice and freedom at certain "superior" anthropo-
logical stages, it's because we will also find them at the most
elementary strata of machinic concatenations. But the notions
of elements and complexity are susceptible here to being brutal-
ly inverted. Those that are most differentiated and undifferentiated coexist within the same chaos which, at infinite speed,
plays its virtual registers — one against the other and one with
the other. The machinic-technical world, at the "terminal" of
which present-day humanity structures itself, is barricaded by

horizons of constants and the limitation of the infinite velocities of chaos (the speed of light, the cosmological horizon of the Big Bang, Planck's constant and the elementary quantum of action in quantum physics, the impossibility of going below absolute zero...). But, this very same world of semiotic constraints is doubled, tripled and infinitised by other worlds which under certain conditions seek only to bifurcate out of their Universes of virtuality and engender new fields of the possible.

Just as scientific machines constantly modify our cosmic frontiers, so do the machines of desire and aesthetic creation. As such, they hold an eminent place within assemblages of subjectivation, themselves called to relieve our old social machines which are incapable of keeping up with the efflorescence of machinic revolutions that shatter our epoch.

Rather than adopting a reticent attitude with respect to the immense machinic revolution sweeping the planet (at the risk of destroying it) or of clinging onto traditional systems of value — with the pretence of re-establishing transcendence — the movement of progress, or if one prefers, the movement of process, will endeavour to reconcile values and machines. Values are immanent to machines. The life of machinic Fluxes is not only manifested through cybernetic feedback; it is also correlative to a promotion of incorporeal Universes stemming from an enunciative Territorial incarnation, from a valorising consciousness of being. Machinic autopoiesis asserts itself as a non-human for-itself through zones of partial proto-subjectivation and it deploys a for-others under the double modality of a "horizontal" eco-systemic alterity (the machinic systems position themselves in a rhizome of reciprocal dependence) and phylogenetic alterity (situating each actual machinic stasis at the conjunction of a passéist filiation and a Phylum of future mutations). All systems of value — religious, aesthetic, scientific, ecosophic... — install themselves at this machinic interface between the necessary actual and the possibilist virtual. Thus Universes of value constitute incorporeal enunciators of abstract machinic complexions compossible with discursive realities. The consistency of these zones of proto-subjectivation is then only assured inasmuch as they are embodied, with more or less intensity, in nodes of finitude, Territories of chaosmic grasping, which guarantee, moreover, their possible recharging with processual complexity. Thus a double enunciation: finite, territorialised and incorporeal, infinite.

Nevertheless, these constellations of Universes of value do not constitute Universals. The fact that they are tied into singular existential Territories effectively confers upon them a power of heterogenesis, that is, of opening onto singularising, irreversible processes of necessary differentiation. How does this machinic heterogenesis, which differentiates each colour of being — which makes, for example, from the plane of consistency of a philosophical concept a world quite different from the plane of reference of the scientific function or the plane of aesthetic composition — end up being reduced to the capitalistic homogenesis of generalised equivalence, which leads to all values being valued by the same thing, all appropriative territories being related to the same economic instrument of power, and all existential riches succumbing to clutches of exchange value? The sterile opposition between use value and exchange value will here be relinquished in favour of an axiological complexion including all the machinic modalities of valorisation: the values of desire, aesthetic values, ecological, economic values ... Capitalistic value which generally subsumes the ensemble of these machinic surplus values, proceeds with a reterritorialising attack, based on the primacy of economic and monetary semiotics, and corresponds to a sort of general implosion of all existential Territories. In fact, capitalistic value is neither separate nor tangential to systems of valorisation; it constitutes their deathly heart, corresponding to the crossing of the ineffable limit between a controlled, chaosmic deterritorialisation — under the aegis of social, aesthetic and analytical practices — and a vertiginous collapse into the black hole of the aleatory, understood as a paroxysmically binary reference, implacably dissolving the whole consistency of Universes of value which would claim to escape capitalistic law. It is thus only abusively that one could put economic determinations in a primary position with respect to social relations and productions of subjectivity. Economic law, like juridical law, must be deducted from the ensemble of Universes of value, for whose collapse it continually strives. Its reconstruction, from the scattered debris of planned economies and neo-liberalism and according to new ethico-political finalities (ecosophy) calls for, in contradistinction, an untiring renewal of the consistency of machinic assemblages of valorisation.

1   Norbert Wiener, *Cybernetics, or, Control and communication in the animal and the machine*, Technology Press, Cambridge, Mass., 1948.

2   Cf. Pierre Lévy, *Les Technologies de l'intelligence*, La Découverte, Paris, 1990, *Plissé fractal. Ideographie dynamique* (memoire d'habilitation à diriger des recherches en sciences de l'information et de la communication) et *L'idéographie dynamique*, La Découverte, Paris, 1991.

3   F. Varela op. cit.

4   Leibniz, in his concern to render homogeneous the infinitely large and the infinitely small, thought that the living machine, which he assimilated to a divine machine, continued to be a machine in its smallest parts until infinity (which would not be the case with a machine made by the art of men), in *Monadologie*, pp.178-9, Delagrave, Paris, 1962.

5   M. Augé, "Le fétiche et son objet" in *L'Objet en psychanalyse*, presented by Maud Mannoni, Denoël, "L'espace analytique," Paris, 1986.

6   Ibid.
7   Martin Heidegger, *Basic Writings*, edited by David Farrell Krell,
    Harper, San Francisco, 1977, p.298.

3

Schizoanalytic metamodelisation

Psychoanalysis is in crisis; it is bogged down in routine practices and ossified conceptions. Social movements are also at an impasse due to the collapse of communist regimes and the conversion of social-democrats to liberalism. In each case, individual and collective subjectivity lack modelisation. And it is quite obvious that neither Freudianism, even when revisited by structuralism, nor Freudo-Marxism, have anything worthwhile to offer at this level. In fact, an immense site of theoretical recomposition and invention of new practices has opened up. I have tried to show that questioning subjectivity's foundation on personological Universals, structural mathemes, biological or economic infrastructures, involves a redefinition of machinism. From now on the machine will be conceived in opposition to structure, the latter being associated with a feeling of eternity and the former with an awareness of finitude, precariousness, destruction and death.

Beneath the diversity of beings, no univocal ontological plinth is given, rather there is a plane of machinic interfaces. Being crystallises through an infinity of enunciative assemblages associating actualised, discursive components (material and indicative Fluxes, machinic Phylums) with non-discursive, virtual components (incorporeal Universes and existential Territories). Thus the singular points of view on being, with their precariousness, uncertainty and creative aspects take precedence over the fixity of structures so distinctive of universalist visions. In order to establish an intensive bridge between these actual and virtual functions we are inclined to postulate the existence of a deterministic chaos animated by infinite velocities. It is out of this chaos that complex compositions, which are capable of being slowed down in energetico-spatio-temporal coordinates or category systems, constitute themselves.

Rather than beginning with automatic systems of articulation between a plane of Expression and a plane of Content, we will stress the partial operators of their assemblage. For example, the mechanical aspect of the linguistic double articulation between signifying, monemic unities and non-signifying, phonemic unities will be replaced by abstract machines which traverse these two heterogeneous registers and are capable of bifurcation and the production of new associations. It is not evident that Universes of value function in concert with semiotic machines, or that semiotic machines combine with concrete machines, that existential Territories cut out points of view on the world.... By making assemblages of enunciation open, chaotically determined, the concatenation of the four ontological functions of Universe, machinic Phylum, Flux and Territory, preserve their pragmatic processuality. The structuralist mode wanted to bracket out the problematics of the signified, the icon, the Imago and the imaginary, to the advantage of syntagmatic articulations. Attention was focused on interactional, structural mechanics, which supposedly animated the phenomenal landscape. Thus the points of ontological crystallisation emerging from this landscape were lost from sight. The phonological, gestural, spatial, musical...discursivities, all annexed by the same signifying economy, had to have absolute control over the contents they were supposed to divide into discrete paradigmatic figures. But what gives consistency to these discursive systems, what authorises the erection of enunciative monads should be sought on the side of Content; that is, on the side of this existential function which, taking support from certain discursive links, diverts them from their signifying, denotational and propositional incidences, making them play the role of a refrain of ontological affirmation.

The assemblage of the four ontological functions. *functires*

	Expression actual (discursive)	**Content** virtual enunciative nuclei (non-discursive)
possible	Φ = machinic discursivity	**U** = incorporeal complexity
real	**F** = energetico-spatio- temporal discursivity	**T** = chaosmic incarnation

The functions F, Φ, T, U have the task of conferring a diagrammatic, conceptual status (pragmatic cartography) on the virtual enunciative nuclei stuck within manifest Expression. Their matricial concatenation should preserve, as much as possible, their radical heterogeneity, which can only be sensed through a discursive, phenomenological approach. They are described here as metamodelisers to indicate that their primary purpose is to take account of the way in which the diverse existing systems of modelisation (religious, metaphysical, scientific, psychoanalytic, animistic, neurotic...) nearly always skirt around the problem of self-referential enunciation. Schizoanalysis does not thus choose one modelisation to the exclusion of another. Within the diverse cartographies in action in a given situation, it tries to make nuclei of virtual autopoiesis discernible, in order to actualise them, by transversalising them, in conferring on them an operative diagrammatism (for example, by a change in the material of Expression), in making them themselves operative within modified assemblages, more open, more processual, more deterritorialised. Schizoanalysis, rather than moving in the direction of reductionist modelisations which simplify the complex, will work towards its complexification, its processual enrichment, towards the consistency of its virtual lines of bifurcation and differentiation, in short towards its ontological heterogeneity.

The location of nuclei of partial life, of that which can give an enunciative consistency to phenomenal multiplicities, is not a matter of a pure objective description. A monad's knowledge of being-in-the-world, of a sphere of for-itself, implies a pathic apprehension which escapes energetico-spatio-temporal coordinates. Knowledge here is first of all existential transference, non-discursive transitivism. The enunciation of this transference always occurs through the diversion of a narration whose primary function is not to engender a rational explanation but to promote complex refrains, supports of an intensive, memorial persistence and an event-centred consistency. It is only through mythical narratives (religious, fantasmatic, etc.) that the existential function accedes to discourse. But this discourse is not a simple epiphenomenon; it is the stake of ethico-political strategies of avoidance of enunciation. The four ontological functions, like safety barriers or warning lights, have the task of making visible the stakes of these strategies.

For example, the incorporeal Universes of classical Antiquity which were associated with a polytheistic compromise relating to a multitude of clanic and ethnic Territorialities, underwent a radical reshaping with the trinitary revolution of Christianity, indexed on the refrain of the sign of the cross, which will recentre not only the ensemble of social, existential Territories, but also the corporeal, mental, familial assemblages, on the unique existential Territory of Christic incarnation and crucifixion. This extraordinary attack of subjective subjection obviously goes far beyond purely theological considerations! The new subjectivity of guilt, contrition, body markings and sexuality, of redemptive mediation, is also an essential piece of the new social apparatuses, the new machines of subjection which had to construct themselves from the debris of the late Roman Empire and the reterritorialisations of feudal and urban orders yet to come.

Closer to us, the mythico-conceptual narrative of Freudianism has effected a reshaping of the four ontological quadrants. A whole dynamic and topical machinery of repression governs the economy of the Fluxes of the libido; while a zone of enunciative nuclei (that the clinical approach had bypassed) — of an oneiric, sexual, neurotic and infantile order relating to the lapsus and jokes — invades the right hand side of our picture. The Unconscious presented as a universe of non-contradiction, of the heterogenesis of opposites, envelops the manifest Territories of the symptom, whose tendency towards autonomisation, autopoietic, pathic and pathogenic repetition threatens the unity of the self. And this will reveal itself moreover during the history of the analytical clinic to be increasingly precarious, indeed fractalised. Freudian cartography is not only descriptive; it is inseparable from the pragmatics of transference and interpretation. In any event, I would argue that it should be disengaged from a significational perspective and understood as a conversion of expressive means and as a mutation of ontological textures releasing new lines of the possible

— and this from the simple fact of putting into place new assemblages of listening and modelisation. The dream, as an object of renewed interest, recounted as a story concealing keys to the Unconscious, put through the screen of free association, undergoes a profound mutation. Just as after the revolution of the Ars Nova in Fourteenth Century Italy music will no longer be heard in the same way within the European cultural atmosphere, so too the nature of the dream and oneiric activity will intrinsically change within their new referential assemblage. And, at the same time, a multitude of psychopathological refrains will no longer be lived, and consequently modelised, in the same way. And the obsessive who washes his hands a hundred times a day exacerbates his solitary anguish within the context of a profoundly modified Universe of reference.

With the invention of the analytic apparatus, Freudian modelisation brought about a clear enrichment in the production of subjectivity, an enlargement of its referential constellations, a new pragmatic opening. But it quickly encountered limits with its familial and universalising conceptions, with its stereotyped practice of interpretation, but above all with its inability to go beyond linguistic semiology. While psychoanalysis conceptualises psychosis through its vision of neurosis, schizoanalysis approaches all modalities of subjectivation in light of the mode of being in the world of psychosis. Because nowhere more than here is the ordinary modelisation of everyday existence so denuded; the "axioms of daily life" stand in the way of the a-signifying function, the degree zero of all possible modelisation. With neurosis, symptomatic matter continues to bathe in the environment of dominant significations while with psychosis the world of standardised Dasein loses its consistency. Alterity, as such, becomes the primary question. For example, what finds itself fragilised, cracked up, schizzed, in délire or hallucinating when confronted with the status of the objective world, is the point of view of the other in me, the recognised body in articulation with the lived body and the felt body; these are the normalised coordinates of alterity which give their foundation to sensible evidence.

Psychosis is not a structural object but a concept; it is not an irremovable essence but a machination which always starts up again during any encounter with the one who will become, after the event, the psychotic. Thus here the concept is not an entity closed in on itself, but the abstract, machinic incarnation of alterity at the point of extreme precariousness; it is the indelible mark that everything in this world can break down at any time. The Unconscious is intimately connected with the concept: it too is an incorporeal construction which takes possession of subjectivity at the point of its emergence. But it is a concept which at every moment risks becoming clogged up, and which must be constantly cleared of the cultural scoria which threatens to reterritorialise it. It requires reactivating, machinic recharging, due to the virulence of events which set subjectivity into action. The schizo fracture is the royal road of access to the emergent fractality of the Unconscious. What could be called the schizo reduction goes beyond all the eidetic reductions of phenomenology — it leads to an encounter with the a-signifying refrains which give back to the narrative, which recast in artifice, existential narrativity and alterity, albeit delirious ones. Note the curious chassé-croisé between psychoanalysis and phenomenology: while the first essentially lacked psychotic alterity (in particular, because of its reifying conceptions about identification and its incapacity to think intensive becomings), the second, although having produced the best descriptions of psychosis, did not know how to bring to light, through it, the foundational role of narrative modelisation, the medium for the uncircumventable existential function of the

refrain — phantasmatic, mythic, novelistic.... Here we find the
source of Tertullian's paradox: it's because it is impossible for
the son to be dead, buried and resuscitated, that these facts
must be held to be certain. It's because in many respects
Freudian theory is mythical that it can trigger refrains of
mutant subjectivation.

In place of the traditional logic of sets described univocally
(where one always knows without ambiguity whether or not
an element is included) schizoanalytic modelisation substitutes
an onto-logic, a machinics of existence whose object is not circumscribed within fixed, extrinsic coordinates; and this object
can, at any moment, extend beyond itself, proliferate or abolish
itself with the Universes of alterity with which it is compossible.
As I have already indicated, the work of Daniel Stern clarifies
these kinds of transversalist entities in the context of the development of the interpersonal relations of infants. The ethology
of a child's preverbal phases reveals a psychical world where
family characters do not yet constitute autonomised structural
poles, but disclose, in my own terminology, multiple, dislocated
and entangled, existential Territories and incorporeal Universes.
The maternal, paternal, fraternal Universes — territories of the
self — agglomerate into a kind of phenomenon of an autopoietic snowball which renders the development of the sense of self
and the sense of the other totally interdependent.

A primary assemblage of subjectivation, which Daniel Stern
calls the emergent self, is already apparent at birth and is
deployed until the second month. Outside of any linguistic or
corporeal distinctivity, it develops a Universe of early perceptions of forms, intensities, of movement and number. These
abstract and amodal forms install themselves transversally in
the diverse perceptual registers; already at birth the infant has
the extraordinary capacity of seeing and feeling what it hears

(and reciprocally). The emergent self — atmospheric, pathic, fusional, transitivist — ignores the oppositions of subject-object, self-other and of course masculine-feminine. It is the reign of an absolute maternitude, which won't buy into any Oedipal triangulation, but which will be perhaps after all (*nachträglich*) the elective site of a schizo brother-sister incest. As a Universe of emergence, a sensitive plate registering all incorporeal becomings, the emergent self can in no way be assimilated to a psychogenetic phase, such as the oral phase. First of all because it is not a phase, since it will persist in parallel with other self formations and will haunt the adult's poetic, amorous and oneiric experiences. Furthermore, because the orality it puts to work is not passively physiological or reducible to a question of pressure, source, goal and drive object, it is a partial nucleus of subjectivation, actively machinic, opening onto the most heterogeneous Universes of reference. For example, the fantasm of a devouring orality or of a return to the maternal breast refers to a mother who is neither real, imaginary, nor symbolic but who is cosmic becoming; it is a Universe of processual emergence as much as of abolition. For all that, we are not in the reign of Jungian universal Imagos or mythological entities such as Gaia or Chronos. The Universes of which the mouth and the breast are the refrain-operators are constellated in a composite and heterogenetic way: they constitute singular events.

Between the age of two months and six months, the core self confers its auto-coherence to the body proper and to the corporeal schema. The proprioceptive and exteroceptive givens become complementary, whilst sensory-motor integration develops in parallel to inter-relations with the milieu. A Territory of action, of physical totalisation, of the location of affect and of personal proto-history is established and consolidated. The potential fragilisation of this Universe of corporeality will manifest itself later in the form of catatonia, hysterical paralysis and the feeling of derealisation or paranoid states. We also find it at the root of another figure of death — the death of the body, the cadaver, organic decomposition — which prevails in obsessional neurosis.

The constitution of the subjective-self between seven and fifteen months is correlative to the structuration of affectivity. A dialectic of attunement is established between affects that are sharable with others and those that are not. There is a recognition of the fact that the other can experience something that the subject experiences for itself. It is at the heart of this proto-social and still pre-verbal Universe that familial, ethnic, urban, etc., traits are transmitted (let's call it the Cultural Unconscious). This subjective territoriality is crowned by the designation of self identity (name and pronoun) in the presence of the mirror, at about eighteen months.

The verbal self appears from about two years of age, when linguistic significations are shared with others. It deploys the structural scene of personological identities and familial complexes, with their games of identification, rivalry, conflict, negativism, denial, and their anal and educative disciplines, their prohibitions, their investments in transgression and punishment.... It will be relayed by the scriptural self associated with school assemblages, then to the self of puberty, with the intrusion of genital components, then to the self of adolescent phases, to the professional self, etc. All the Universes of reference in action are superimposed in a kind of incorporeal existential agglomeration. When one of these Universes foregrounds itself, there will not be, strictly speaking, repression of the others, but rather a placing in reserve, in latency, possibly accompanied with a loss of consistency of the contextual constellation; and this can in no way be inserted within a topos, nor balanced within an energetic economy. Any metaphorical representation of the drive, whether topical, dynamic or energetic risks arbitrarily deforming the aporetic character of the crystallisation of these existential Territories, which are at once incorporeal, intensive and multicomponential. The lapsus, for example in this perspective is not the conflictual expression of a repressed Content but the positive, indexical manifestation of a Universe trying to find itself, which comes to knock at the window like a magic bird.

Schizoanalysis obviously does not consist in miming schizophrenia, but in crossing, like it, the barriers of non-sense which prohibit access to a-signifying nuclei of subjectivation, the only way to shift petrified systems of modelisation. It implies an optimal enlargement of pragmatic entrances into Unconscious formations. Autism, for example, no longer being linked exclusively to an infantile regression of the maternal era, will be accessible to interventions other than those of transference focused directly on the body and projective identifications. Indeed, its chaosmic Universe can be constellated with many other Imagos besides those of the personological mother, with vegetal, animal, cosmic or machinic...becomings. The psychotic complex is thus not the exclusive concern of verbal communication and individuated transference. The treatment of a psychotic, in the context of institutional psychotherapy, works with a renewed approach to transference, focused henceforth on parts of the body, on a constellation of individuals, on a group, on an institutional ensemble, a machinic system, a semiotic economy, etc. (grafts of transference), and conceived as desiring becoming, that is to say, pathic existential intensity, impossible to circumscribe as a distinct entity. The objective of such a therapeutic approach would be to increase as much as possible the range of means offered in the recomposition of a patient's corporeal, biological, psychical and social Territories.

To this effect it will engage multiple semiotic vectors relating to corporeality, gesturality, posturality, the traits of faciality and spatiality which are connected to the levels of preverbal assemblages described by Daniel Stern. Treated as an ensemble of autopoietic and transversalist social machines, the caring institution becomes a field propitious to an ability to discern these vectors which intersect with individuated subjectivity, which work it despite itself.

Consider, for example, the institutional sub-ensemble that constitutes the kitchen at La Borde Clinic. It combines highly heterogeneous social, subjective and functional dimensions. This Territory can close in on itself, become the site of stereotyped attitudes and behaviour, where everyone mechanically carries out their little refrain. But it can also come to life, trigger an existential agglomeration, a drive machine — and not simply of an oral kind, which will have an influence on the people who participate in its activities or just passing through. The kitchen then becomes a little opera scene: in it people talk, dance and play with all kinds of instruments, with water and fire, dough and dustbins, relations of prestige and submission. As a place for the preparation of food, it is the centre of exchange of material and indicative Fluxes and prestations of every kind. But this metabolism of Flux will only have transferential significance on the condition that the whole apparatus functions effectively as a structure which welcomes the preverbal components of the psychotic patients. This resource of ambience, of contextual subjectivity, is itself indexed to the degree of openness (coefficient of transversality) of this institutional sub-ensemble to the rest of the institution. The semiotisation of a fantasm — for example the chef who reincarnates "Père Lustucru"[1] — therefore depends on external operators. The proper functioning of the kitchen from this point of view is inseparable from its articulation with the other partial nuclei of subjectivation in the institution (the menu committee, the daily activities information sheet, the pastry workshop, greenhouse, garden, the bar, sports activities, the meeting between the cooks and a doctor with respect to the patients they are working with...) The psychotic who approaches an institutional sub-ensemble, like the kitchen, therefore traverses a well-worked zone of enunciation which can sometimes be closed in on itself and subjected to roles and functions, or find itself in direct contact with Universes of alterity which help the psychotic out of his existential entrapment. It is less by way of voluntary decision than by induction of an unconscious collective assemblage that the psychotic is led to take the initiative, to accept responsibility. Note that collective is not here synonymous with group; it is a description which subsumes on one hand elements of human intersubjectivity, and on the other pre-personal, sensitive and cognitive modules, micro-social processes and elements of the social imaginary. It operates in the same way on non-human subjective formations (machinic, technical and economic). It is therefore a term which is equivalent to heterogeneous multiplicity. Thus in the context of institutional psychotherapy what is called too schematically the care-giver/care-receiver relationship is broken down into heterogeneous dimensions: 1) of psychiatric knowledge and technicalities that concern clearly defined problems from a nosographic perspective; 2) of social activation within permanently worked collective Territories; 3) of pathic apprehension of the existential differences borne by psychotic Universes. Knowledge establishes a distance which collective social life tends to dissolve while the existential caesura brings about a far more intimate and enigmatic rapprochement. Training in this domain consists in articulating, in a relatively harmonious way, these three dimensions; the moment of the return to the socius and technical skills, after the chaosmic submersion in psychosis, being by far the most problematic.

The most autistic psychical world is not in itself lacking in alterity. It is simply engaged in a constellation of Universes disconnected from the dominant assemblages of sociality. Lines can be thrown to the psychotic by mediations which will give consistency to certain of these components of Universes, or by the aggregation of other components which did not previously exist. (Through the introduction of materials of expression unknown to the subject, for example, relating to the plastic arts, video, music, theatre or quite simply...cooking!). Schizoanalytic cartography consists in the ability to discern those components lacking in consistency or existence. But it is a question here of an essentially precarious undertaking, of a continual creation, which does not have the benefit of any pre-established theoretical support. The enunciative emergence of the kitchen at La Borde, to stay with this example, can lead it to take on the role of partial analyser, without any guarantee in time. The autopoietic character of such an instance calls for a permanent renewal of the assemblage, a verification of its capacity to welcome a-signifying singularities — unbearable patients, insoluble conflicts — a constant readjustment of its transversalist opening onto the outside world. Only the network of nuclei of partial enunciation — comprising groups, meetings, workshops, responsibilities, spontaneous constellations and individual initiatives — could arguably hold the title of institutional analyser. The work of the psychotherapist in the office is only a link in this complex apparatus; individuated transference is but one element of the generalised transference already evoked. Just as the schizo has broken moorings with subjective individuation, the analysis of the Unconscious should be recentred on the non-human processes of subjectiva-

tion that I call machinic, but which are more than human —
superhuman in a Nietzschean sense.

This novel type of procedure is not reserved for the analysis
of psychotics but is also applicable to neurotics, psychopaths,
normopaths — following Jean Oury's felicitous expression. It
both puts into question future analytical apparatuses in the
domain of pedagogy, the life of the neighbourhood, the ecology
of retirement — in a whole field of molecular revolutions; and it
works towards an escape from contemporary social desertification. The stakes of a metamodelising theoretical recomposition
of analysis are accordingly raised. They primarily involve a
repudiation of the universalist and transcendent concepts of
psychoanalysis which constrain and sterilise the apprehension
of incorporeal Universes and singularising and heterogenetic
becomings. In this respect, the Lacanian concept of the
Signifier seems to me to be particularly poorly adapted to car-
tographise psychosis; it is even worse for the machinic forms of
subjectivity which develop from the mass media, informatics,
the new telematics and the inflation of Paul Virilio's "dromos-
pheric" velocities of exchange, displacement and communication. The Lacanian Signifier homogenises the various semiotics, it loses the multidimensional character of many of them.
Its fundamental linearity, inherited from Saussurian structuralism, does not allow it to apprehend the pathic, non discursive, autopoietic character of partial nuclei of enunciation. One
indicative topos refers to another indicative topos, without the
trans-topical dimension of agglomeration — which characterise intensive Territories — ever emerging.

Let us illustrate these remarks with the Lacanian rereading
of Freud's famous observation of the game of an eighteen
month old child, which consisted in throwing, out of its cur-
tain-edged bed, a reel attached to the end of a string, accompa-
nying its disappearance with the sound "Oooo" which Freud

translated into adult German by the word "*Fort*" (gone) and its reappearance by "*Da*" (there).[2] Freud thought that with this Fort-Da refrain, the child incessantly replayed the departure, absence and return of its mother. Above all, he put emphasis on the first sequence of rejection, which he considered more important and of a painful character. He associated this kind of pleasure in repetition (peculiar to childhood, according to him — whereas adults would be more inclined towards the desire for novelty) to the repetition, for example, of accident dreams one finds in some traumatic neuroses, or the indefinite repetition of oppressive affects in psychoanalytic transference. He broadly referred it to what he called the compulsion to repeat (*Wiederholungszwang*) at work in sadism, masochism, ambivalence, aggressivity and in the majority of neuroses. This compulsion manifested an irrepressible tendency (that he often called demonic) towards the complete discharge of excitation and the extinction of tensions and conflicts. His economy would no longer respond to the pleasure principle — which tends towards the substitution of an agreeable state for an unpleasant one — since it would repeat to infinity a disagreeable state. It would instead correspond to the submission of the pleasure principle to the death drive, namely, to a presumed tendency of life to return by itself to an inorganic state — the life drives being no more than a provisional detour from the direction of death. When Lacan evokes the Fort-Da refrain in his *Écrits*, he no longer takes into account the absence of the mother. According to him, it is essentially a matter of an intersection between a play of occultation and an alternative scansion of two phonemes. The wait for the return of the object is constituted as an "anticipating provocation," which takes form "in the symbolic dyad of two elementary exclamations" and announces in the subject "the diachronic integration of the dichotomy of phonemes, whose synchronic structure existing language offers to his assimilation."

While Freud reduces the child's complex game to the lack of the mother and makes it subsidiary to the death drive, Lacan ties it down to the signifying discursivity of "existing language." Which does not spare this innocent refrain from being marked by death — although in a more Hegelian way, since Lacan comments, with respect to this symbol, that it "manifests itself first of all as murder of the thing, and (that) this death constitutes in the subject the eternalisation of his desire."[3] Thus the reel, the string, the curtain, the observer's gaze, all the singular characteristics of the assemblage of enunciation fall into the trap of the Signifier. Rather than recognising that with this refrain the child encounters unforeseen Universes of the possible, with incalculable, virtual repercussions, Lacan defines it as "a point of insertion of a symbolic order that pre-exists the infantile subject and in accordance with which he will have to structure himself."[4] The structure, here, precedes and envelops the machine in an operation that strips it of all its autopoietic and creative characteristics. The symbolic order weighs down like a deterministic lead cape, like a deathly fate, on the possible bifurcations of incorporeal Universes. The eternisation of desire, mentioned by Lacan, is a petrification — moreover, in a subsequent phrase he suggests that the sepulchre is the first symbol by which one recognises humanity.

Unlike Freud, schizoanalysis doesn't make the Fort-Da refrain depend on a feeling of frustration with regard to the mother and on universal principles of life and death; nor like Lacan on a transcendent signifying order. It considers it as a desiring machine, working towards the assemblage of the verbal self — in symbiosis with the other assemblages of the emergent self, the nuclear self and the subjective self — and thereby inaugurating a new mastery of the object, of touch, of a spatiality dissociated from Winnicott's transitional space.[5] As Freud observed, Fort-Da is found in other behaviours; it can be expressed in relation to the effective absence of the mother or in a child's game with its own image in the mirror that it makes appear and disappear. It is, in fact, a matter of a rich, multivalent, heterogenetic machine that can neither be legitimately fixed to a maternal-oral stasis, nor to a language stasis, although they incontestably participate in it. It is all these things at the same time and many others besides! We have to choose here between a mechanical conception of deathly repetition and a machinic conception of processual opening. There is an inspired element in Freud's intuition about a relation between the automatism of repetition and a death drive, that I would prefer to put down to the desire for destruction that inhabits all desiring machines. There is no encounter or relation of intimate intrication between two distinct drives, Eros and Thanatos, but a coming and going at infinite speed between chaos and complexity. Fort is chaosmic submersion; Da the mastery of a differentiated complexion. The drive is not "conservative" as the death drive would be (this is how Freud liked to describe it). The insistence on failure, the eternal return of the splinter in the flesh, the appearance of demonic fatality that sometimes occurs in neurotic "bad-luck" stems from the persistence of a loss of consistency of the assemblage, or if one prefers, from the consistency of a loss of consistency (reterritorialisation). The submersion in chaosmic immanence is always ready to exploit the slightest weaknesses. Its presence haunts, with more or less intensity, unstable situations — intolerable absence, bereavement, jealousy, organic fragilisation, cosmic vertigo.... The rituals of exorcism brought to bear on it can become refrains of fixation, reification, tenacious fidelity to pain or unhappiness. Surely here we are far from the child's proba-

bly happy Fort-Da refrain. The Unconscious of the dualist
hypothesis of drives of life and death, like that of the transcendence of the Signifier — the murderer of the "things" of context
— petrify chaosmic abolition, by making it lose its immanence;
they transform it into deathly negativity, into a cadaverous
object. It is true that a certain capitalistic, reductionist use of
language leads it to the state of a signifying linearity of discrete
binary entities which smother, silence, disempower and kill the
polysemic qualities of a Content reduced to the state of a neutral "referent." Isn't the task of analysis precisely to recharge
Expression with semiotic heterogeneity and to run counter to
the disenchantment, demystification and depoetisation of the
contemporary world denounced by Max Weber?

1   [Père Lustucru is a character in an advertisement for pasta.]
2   Sigmund Freud, *Beyond the Pleasure Principle*, in *On
    Metapsychology: The Theory of Psychoanalysis*, The Pelican Freud
    Library Vol. 11, Penguin, Harmondsworth, 1984, p.284.
3   Jacques Lacan, *Ecrits*, trans. Alan Sheridan, Tavistock, London,
    1977, pp.103-4.
4   Ibid., p.234.
5   *La Psychanalyse*, Tome V, PUF, Paris, 1959.[See D.W. Winnicott,
    Playing and Reality, Tavistock Publications, London, 1971.]

4

Schizo chaosmosis

"Normality" in the light of délire, technical logic in the light of Freudian primary processes — a pas de deux towards chaos in the attempt to delineate a subjectivity far from dominant equilibria, to capture its virtual lines of singularity, emergence and renewal — eternal Dionysian return or paradoxical Copernican inversion to be prolonged by an animist revival? At the very least an originary fantasm of a modernity constantly under scrutiny and without hope of postmodern remission. It's always the same aporia: madness enclosed in its strangeness, reified in alterity beyond return, nevertheless inhabits our ordinary, bland apprehension of the world. But we must go further: chaotic vertigo, which finds one of its privileged expressions in madness, is constitutive of the foundational intentionality of the subject-object relation. Psychosis starkly reveals an essential source of being-in-the-world.

What takes precedence, in fact, in the mode of being of psychosis — but also, according to other modalities, in the "emergent self" of infancy (Daniel Stern) or in aesthetic creation — is the irruption, at the forefront of the subjective scene, of a real "anterior" to discursivity; a real whose pathic consistency liter-

ally leaps at your throat. Must we think of this real as fixed, petrified and rendered catatonic by a pathological accident, or that
it was in fact there for all time — past and future — awaiting
the activation of a presumed symbolic castration as the sanc-
tion of foreclosure? Perhaps it is necessary to straddle these two
perspectives: it was already there as an open virtual reference,
and it arises correlatively as a production sui generis of a singular event.

Structuralists were too hasty in positioning the Real of psychosis topically in relation to the Imaginary of neurosis and the
Symbolic of normality. What did they achieve? In erecting universal mathemes of the Real, the Imaginary and the Symbolic
— considered as a unity each for themselves — they reified and
reduced the complexity of what was at stake, the crystallisation
of real-virtual Universes assembled from a multiplicity of imaginary Territories and semiotised in the most diverse ways. The
real complexions, for example, those of everyday life, dreams,
passion, délire, depression and aesthetic experience do not all
have the same ontological colour. What is more, they are not
passively endured, nor mechanically articulated or dialectically
triangulated to other instances. Once certain thresholds of
autopoietic consistency have been crossed, these real complexions start to work for themselves, constituting nuclei of partial
subjectivation. Note that their expressive instruments (of semiotisation, encoding, catalysis, moulding, resonance, identification) cannot be reduced to a single signifying economy. The
practice of institutional psychotherapy has taught us the diversity of modalities of agglomeration of these multiple, real or virtual stases: those of the body and the soma, the self and other,
lived space and temporal refrains, the family socius and the
socius artificially elaborated so as to open up other fields of the
possible, those of psychotherapeutic transference or even those
immaterial Universes relating to music, plastic forms, animal

becomings, vegetal becomings, machinic becomings....
The complexions of the psychotic real, in their clinical
emergence, constitute a privileged exploratory path for other
ontological modes of production in that they disclose aspects of
excess and limit experiences. Psychosis thus not only haunts
neurosis and perversion but also all the forms of normality.
Psychotic pathology is specific in that for x reasons the expect-
ed toings-and-froings and the "normal" polyphonic relations
between the different modes of bringing into being of subjective
enunciation see their heterogeneity compromised by repetition
— the exclusive insistence of an existential stasis that I describe
as chaosmic and which is capable of assuming all the hues of a
schizo-paranoiac-manic-epileptoid, etc., spectrum. Everywhere
else this stasis is only apprehended by way of avoidance, displacement, misrecognition, distortion, overdetermination, ritu-
alisation. In these conditions, psychosis could be defined as a
hypnosis of the real. Here a sense of being-in-itself is established
before any discursive scheme, uniquely positioned across an
intensive continuum whose distinctive traits are not percepti-
ble by an apparatus of representation but by a pathic, existential absorption, a pre-egoic, pre-identificatory agglomeration.
As long as the schizophrenic is installed at the centre of this
gaping and chaotic opening, paranoiac délire manifests an
unbounded will to take possession of it. For their part, passional
délires (Sérieux, Capgras and de Clérambault) would display a
grasping intentionality in a less closed, more processual chaosmosis. The perversions already involve the signifying recomposition of poles of alterity which are bestowed from the outside
with the power to incarnate controlled chaosmosis, teleguided
by fantasmatic scenarios. As for neurotics, they present all the
variants of avoidance evoked above, beginning with the simplest and most reifying, that of phobia, followed by hysteria,
which forges from them substitutes in social space and the

body, ending with obsessional neurosis which, for its part, secretes a perpetual temporal "différance" (Derrida), an indefinite procrastination.

This theme of chaosmic immanence and these nosographic variations need to be developed; I have only introduced them here in order to suggest the idea that the ontological apprehension belonging to psychosis is in no way synonymous with simple chaotic degradation, with a trivial increase in entropy. It would be a matter of reconciling chaos and complexity. (It is to Freud's credit that he showed the way in the *Traumdeutung*.) Why describe the homogenesis of ontological referents — and, by extension, the latent homogenesis of other modalities of subjectivation — as chaotic? It's because, all things considered, worlding a complexion of sense always involves taking hold of a massive and immediate ensemble of contextual diversity, a fusion in an undifferentiated, or rather de-differentiated, whole. A world is only constituted on the condition of being inhabited by an umbilical point — deconstructive, detotalisating and deterritorialising — from which a subjective positionality embodies itself. The effects of such a nucleus of chaosmosis is to make the ensemble of differential terms (distinctive oppositions, the poles of discursivity) the object of a generalised connectivity, an indifferent mutability, a systematic dequalification. At the same time, this vacuole of decompression is an autopoietic node on which existential Territories and Incorporeal Universes of reference constantly reaffirm and entangle themselves, demanding and developing consistency. This oscillation at infinite speed between a state of chaotic "grasping" and the deployment of complexions anchored within worldly coordinates takes place before space and time, before the processes of spatialisation and temporalisation. Formations of sense and states of things are thus chaotised in the very movement of the bringing into existence of their complexity. At the source of a world's constitution there is always a certain modality of chaotic discomfort in its organicity, functionality and relations of alterity.

Unlike Freudian metapsychology, we are not going to oppose two antagonistic drives, of life and death, complexity and chaos. The most originary, objectal intentionality defines itself against a background of chaosmosis. And chaos is not pure indifferentiation; it possesses a specific ontological texture. It is inhabited by virtual entities and modalities of alterity which have nothing universal about them. It is not therefore Being in general which irrupts in the chaosmic experience of psychosis, or in the pathic relationship one can enter into with it, but a signed and dated event, marking a destiny, inflecting previously stratified significations. After such a process of dequalification and ontological homogenesis, nothing will be like it was before. But the event is inseparable from the texture of the being brought to light. This is what the psychotic aura attests to when a feeling of catastrophe about the end of the world (François Tosquelles) is associated with an overwhelming feeling of imminent redemption of every possibility or, in other words, the alarming oscillation between a proliferating complexity of sense and total vacuity, a hopeless dereliction of existential chaosmosis.

In the pathic apprehension of délire, dreams and passion, it is essential to realise that the ontological petrification, the existential freezing of the heterogenesis of beings which manifest themselves there according to particular styles, is always latent in other modalities of subjectivation. It is like a freeze-frame which both indicates its basic (or bass) position in the polyphony of chaosmic components, and intensifies its power relative to them. Thus it does not constitute a degree zero of subjectivation, a neutral, passive, deficient, negative point, but an extreme degree of intensification. It is in passing through this chaotic "earthing," this perilous oscillation, that something else becomes possible, that ontological bifurcations and the emergence of coefficients of processual creativity can occur. The fact that the psychotic patient is incapable of a heterogenetic re-establishment does not in itself obviate the richness of ontological experimentation with which he is confronted despite himself. This is why delirious narrativity, as a discursive power finalised by the crystallisation of a Universe of reference or a non-discursive substance, constitutes the paradigm for the construction and reconstruction of mythical, mystical, aesthetic, even scientific, worlds. The existence of chaosmic stases is certainly not the privilege of psychopathology. Their presence can be detected in philosophy — in Pascal or even the most rationalist authors. The Cartesian sequence of generalised doubt — which precedes an encounter of the utmost urgency with the Cogito, to be succeeded by the reunion with God and the refoundation of the world — is akin to this schizo-chaotic reduction: the fact that complexity and alterity are tempted (by the evil demon) to throw in the towel confers on subjectivity the supplementary power of escaping from spatio-temporal coordinates which are otherwise reinforced. More generally, we can see that a collapsus of sense will always be associated with the promotion of a-signifying links of discursivity dedicated to the ontological weaving of an auto-consistent world. The event-centred rupture thus happens at the heart of being and it is from there that it is able to generate new ontological mutations. Distinctive oppositions, syntaxes and semantics relating to codes, signals and signifiers, pursue their rounds — but to the side of their strata of origin. As in délire, signal-systems and semiotics take off. Schizo chaosmosis is a means for the apperception of abstract machines which work transversally to het-

erogeneous strata. The passage through chaosmic homogenesis, which can be a path to complexual heterogenesis (but this
is never mechanically or dialectically guaranteed), does not
constitute a translucent, indifferent zone of being, but an intolerable nucleus of ontological creationism.

By dismantling the ontological heterogenesis which confers
its diversity to the world and its distraction (in Pascal's sense)
to subjectivity, schizo homogenesis exacerbates the transversal
power of chaosmosis, its ability to traverse strata and break
through barriers. Whence the frequently observed capacity of
many schizophrenics to reveal, as if by accident, the best guard-
ed intentions of their interlocutors, to somehow read the
Unconscious like an open book. Complexity released from its
signifying, discursive constraints is embodied in mute, immo-
bile and stupefying, abstract machinic dances. We should be
wary of the simplifying and reifying use of categories such as
autism and dissociation to describe schizo strangeness, the loss
of vital feeling for depression, glischrogeny for epilepsy....
Rather than global and standard deficit alterations of normal
subjectivity, we are actually dealing with modalities of auto-
alterity that are at once plural and singular. I is an other, a
multiplicity of others, embodied at the intersection of partial
components of enunciation, breaching on all sides individuated
identity and the organised body. The cursor of chaosmosis
never stops oscillating between these diverse enunciative
nuclei — not in order to totalise them, synthesise them in a
transcendent self, but in spite of everything, to make a world of
them. So we are in the presence of two types of homogenesis: a
normal and/or neurotic homogenesis, which stops itself from
going too far and for too long into a chaosmic, schizo type of
reduction; and an extreme pathic-pathological homogenesis
leading to a positioning point of worldly complexions, where
not only do components of sensibility (fixed in a time and a

space) and those of affectivity and cognition find themselves conjoined, but also axiological, ethical and aesthetic "charges" as well. On the passive side of schizo ontology we thus find a reductive homogenesis, a loss of colour, flavour and timbre in Universes of reference, but on the active side we find an emergent alterification relieved of the mimetic barriers of the self. Being is affirmed as the responsibility of the other (Levinas) when nuclei of partial subjectivation are constituted in absorption or adsorption with the autonomy and autopoiesis of creative processes.

The point of this is certainly not to make the schizo a hero of the postmodern and above all not to underestimate the weight of systemic components (organic, somatic, imaginary, familial, social) within the psychotic process, but to indicate the effects of inter-componential inhibitions which lead to a stand-off with chaosmic immanence. Social stratifications are set up in a way that avoids, so far as possible, the disquieting strangeness generated by a too marked fixation on chaosmosis. We have to move quickly, we mustn't linger on something that might bog us down: madness, pain, death, drugs, the vertigo of the body without organs, extreme passion.... Of course, all these aspects of existence are the object of a functional awareness by the dominant socius but always as the correlative of an active misrecognition of their chaosmic dimension. The reactive approach to chaosmosis secretes an imaginary of eternity, particularly through the mass media, which misses its essential dimension of finitude: the facticity of being-there, without qualities, without past, without future, in absolute dereliction and yet still a virtual nucleus of complexity without bounds. The eternity of a profoundly infantile adult world that must be opposed to the hyper-lucidity of the child in solitary meditation on the cosmos, or the becoming-child of poetry, music and mystical experience. Only when chaosmosis congeals, implodes

in an abyss of despair, depression and mental derailing —
rather than revitalising complexions of alterity and rekindling
processes of semiotisation — must we of course pose questions
about a recomposition of existential Territories, "grafts of transference," dialogic relays and the invention of all kinds of social
welfare and institutional pragmatics. Not a heroism then of
psychosis but, on the contrary, an unindulgent indexation of
the chaosmic body it carries to incandescence and whose
bruised wrecks are today eaten away by chemotherapy — now
that it has ceased being cultivated in the traditional Asylum,
like so many monstrous flowers.

The delirious primary pulverisation or the grand narrative
constructions of paranoia, the unstable paths healing the
intrusion of the absolute, cannot be put on the same level as
those well socialised systems of defence such as games, sports,
the manias supported by the media, racist phobias.... However,
their mixture is the daily bread of institutional psychotherapy
and schizoanalyses.

It is thus equally from a hotchpotch of banalities, prejudices,
stereotypes, absurd situations — a whole free association of
everyday life — that we have to extricate, once and for all,
these Z or Zen points of chaosmosis, which can only be discovered in nonsense, through the lapsus, symptoms, aporias, the
acting out of somatic scenes, familial theatricalism, or institutional structures. This, I repeat, stems from the fact that chaosmosis is not exclusive to the individuated psyche. We are confronted by it in group life, in economic relations, machinism
(for example, informatics) and even in the incorporeal
Universes of art or religion. In each case, it calls for the reconstruction of an operational narrativity, that is, functioning
beyond information and communication, like an existential
crystallisation of ontological heterogenesis. The fact that the

production of a new real-other-virtual complexion always
results from a rupture of sense, a short circuiting of significations, the manifestation of non-redundant repetition, auto-
affirmative of its own consistency and the promotion of partial
non-"identifiable" nuclei of alterity — which escape identification — condemns the therapist and mental health worker to an
essentially ethical duplicity. One one hand they work in the
register of a heterogenesis of bits and pieces in order to remodel
existential Territories, to forge transitory semiotic components
between blocks of immanence in the process of petrification....
And on the other they can only claim pathic access to the
chaosmic thing — within psychosis and the institution — to
the extent that they in one way or another recreate and reinvent themselves as bodies without organs receptive to non-discursive intensities. Their potential conquests of supplementary
coefficients of heterogenetic liberty, their access to mutant
Universes of reference and their entrance into renewed registers of alterity, depend on their own submersion in homogenetic immanence.

Nosographic categories, psychiatric and psychoanalytic cartographies, necessarily betray the chaosmic texture of psychotic transference. They constitute so many languages, modelisations among others — of délire, the novel, the television serial
— which cannot aspire to any epistemological preeminence.
Nothing more but nothing less! Which is perhaps already a lot,
because they themselves embody roles, points of view and sub-
missive behaviour, and even, why not, liberating processes.
Who speaks the truth? This is no longer the question; but how,
and under what conditions can the best bring about the pragmatics of incorporeal events that will recompose a world and
reinstall processual complexity? The idiosyncratic modelisations grafted onto one-to-one analysis, self-analysis and group

psychotherapy ... always resort to borrowing from specialised languages. Our problematic of chaosmosis and the schizoanalytic escape from the prison of signification is directed — to compensate for these borrowings — towards a necessary a-signifying deconstruction of their discursivity and towards placing their ontological efficacity into a pragmatic perspective.

5

Machinic orality
and virtual ecology

Don't speak with your mouth full, it's very bad manners! You either speak or you eat. Not both at the same time. On one side a differentiated flux — the variety of food taken up in a process of disaggregation, chaotisation, sucked up by an inside of flesh — and on the other side, a flux of elementary articulations — phonological, syntactical, propositional — which invests and constitutes a complex, differentiated outside. But strictly orality is at the intersection. It speaks with its mouth full. It is full of inside and full of outside. In the same space, it is complexity in chaotic involution and simplicity in the process of infinite complexification. A dance of chaos and complexity.

Freud demonstrated that simple objects like milk and shit supported very complex existential Universes: orality, anality, weaving together ways of seeing, symptoms, fantasms.... And we recall one of Lacan's first distinctions between empty and full speech. But full of what? Full of inside and outside, lines of virtuality, fields of the possible. Speech which is not a simple medium of communication, the agent for the transmission of information, but which engenders being-there; speech interface between the cosmic in-itself and the subjective for-itself.

Speech empties itself when it falls into the clutches of scriptural semiologies fixed in the order of law, the control of facts, gestures and feelings. The computer voice — "You have not fastened your seatbelt" — does not leave much room for ambiguity. Ordinary speech tries by contrast to keep alive the presence of at least a minimum of so-called non-verbal semiotic components, where the substances of expression constituted from intonation, rhythm, facial traits and postures, reinforce and take over from each other, superimpose themselves, averting in advance the despotism of signifying circularity. But at the supermarket there is no more time to chat about the quality of a product or haggle for a good price. The necessary and sufficient information has evacuated the existential dimensions of expression. We are not there to exist but to accomplish our duty as consumers.

Would orality constitute a refuge for semiotic polyvocality, a reprise in real time for the emergence of the subject-object relation? Quite frankly too marked an opposition between the oral and the scriptural seems hardly relevant. The oral, even the most quotidian, is overcoded by the scriptural; the scriptural, however highly sophisticated, is worked by the oral. Instead, we will begin with blocks of sensations formed by aesthetic practices before the oral, textual, gestural, postural, plastic ... whose function is to elude significations attached to the trivial perceptions and opinions informing common sentiments. This extraction of deterritorialised percepts and affects from banal perceptions and states of mind takes us from the voice of interior discourse and from self-presence — and from what is most standardised about them — on paths leading to radically mutant forms of subjectivity. A subjectivity of the outside and of wide-open spaces which far from being fearful of finitude — the trials of life, suffering, desire and death — embraces them like a spice essential to the cuisine of life.

Performance art delivers the instant to the vertigo of the emergence of Universes that are simultaneously strange and familiar. It has the advantage of drawing out the full implications of this extraction of intensive, a-temporal, a-spatial, a-signifying dimensions from the semiotic net of quotidianity. It shoves our noses up against the genesis of being and forms, before they get a foothold in dominant redundancies — of styles, schools and traditions of modernity. But it seems to me that this art doesn't so much involve a return to an originary orality as it does a forward flight into machinations and deterritorialised machinic paths capable of engendering mutant subjectivities. What I mean by this is that there is something artificial, constructed, composed — what I call a machinic processuality — in concrete poetry's rediscovery of orality. In a more general way, every aesthetic decentring of points of view, every polyphonic reduction of the components of expression passes through a preliminary deconstruction of the structures and codes in use and a chaosmic plunge into the materials of sensation. Out of them a recomposition becomes possible: a recreation, an enrichment of the world (something like enriched uranium), a proliferation not just of the forms but of the modalities of being. Thus not a Manichean, nostalgic and old fashioned opposition between good orality and wicked scripturality, but a search for enunciative nuclei which would institute new cleavages between other insides and other outsides and which would offer a different metabolism of past-future where eternity will coexist with the present moment.

In our era, aesthetic machines offer us the most advanced models — relatively speaking — for these blocks of sensation capable of extracting full meaning from all the empty signal systems that invest us from every side. It is in underground art that we find some of the most important cells of resistance against the steam-roller of capitalistic subjectivity — the subjectivity of one-dimensionality, generalised equivalence, segregation, and deafness to true alterity. This is not about making artists the new heroes of the revolution, the new levers of History! Art is not just the activity of established artists but of a whole subjective creativity which traverses the generations and oppressed peoples, ghettoes, minorities.... I simply want to stress that the aesthetic paradigm — the creation and composition of mutant percepts and affects — has become the paradigm for every possible form of liberation, expropriating the old scientific paradigms to which, for example, historical materialism or Freudianism were referred. The contemporary world — tied up in its ecological, demographic and urban impasses — is incapable of absorbing, in a way that is compatible with the interests of humanity, the extraordinary technico-scientific mutations which shake it. It is locked in a vertiginous race towards ruin or radical renewal. All the bearings — economic, social, political, moral, traditional — break down one after the other. It has become imperative to recast the axes of values, the fundamental finalities of human relations and productive activity. An ecology of the virtual is thus just as pressing as ecologies of the visible world. And in this regard, poetry, music, the plastic arts, the cinema — particularly in their performance or performative modalities — have an important role to play, with their specific contribution and as a paradigm of reference in new social and analytic practices (psychoanalytic in the broadest sense). Beyond the relations of actualised forces, virtual ecology will not simply attempt to preserve the endangered species of cultural life but equally to engender conditions for the creation and development of unprecedented formations of subjectivity that have never been seen and never felt. This is to say that generalised ecology — or ecosophy — will work as a science of ecosystems, as a bid for political regenera-

tion, and as an ethical, aesthetic and analytic engagement. It
will tend to create new systems of valorisation, a new taste for
life, a new gentleness between the sexes, generations, ethnic
groups, races....

Strange contraptions, you will tell me, these machines of virtuality, these blocks of mutant percepts and affects, half-object
half-subject, already there in sensation and outside themselves
in fields of the possible. They are not easily found at the usual
marketplace for subjectivity and maybe even less at that for art;
yet they haunt everything concerned with creation, the desire
for becoming-other, as well as mental disorder or the passion
for power. Let us try, for the moment, to give an outline of them
starting with some of their principal characteristics.

The assemblages of aesthetic desire and the operators of virtual ecology are not entities which can easily be circumscribed
within the logic of discursive sets. They have neither inside nor
outside. They are limitless interfaces which secrete interiority
and exteriority and constitute themselves at the root of every
system of discursivity. They are becomings — understood as
nuclei of differentiation — anchored at the heart of each
domain, but also between the different domains in order to
accentuate their heterogeneity. A becoming child (for example
in the music of Schumann) extracts childhood memories so as
to embody a perpetual present which installs itself like a
branching, a play of bifurcations between becoming woman,
becoming plant, becoming cosmos, becoming melodic....

These assemblages cannot be located in terms of extrinsic
systems of reference, such as energetico-spatio-temporal coordinates or well-catalogued, semantic coordinates. For all that they
are apprehendable through an awareness of ontological, transitivist, transversalist and pathic consistencies. One gets to know
them not through representation but through affective contam-

ination. They start to exist in you, in spite of you. And not only as crude, undifferentiated affects, but as hyper-complex compositions: "that's Debussy, that's jazz, that's Van Gogh." The paradox which aesthetic experience constantly returns us to is that these affects, as a mode of existential apprehension, are given all at once, regardless, or besides the fact that indicative traits and descriptive refrains are necessary for catalysing their existence in fields of representation. These games of representation possess multiple registers which induce unforeseeable consequences in existential Universes. But whatever their sophistication, a block of percept and affect, by way of aesthetic composition, agglomerates in the same transversal flash the subject and object, the self and other, the material and incorporeal, the before and after.... In short, affect is not a question of representation and discursivity, but of existence. I find myself transported into a Debussyst Universe, a blues Universe, a blazing becoming of Provence. I have crossed a threshold of consistency. Before the hold of this block of sensation, this nucleus of partial subjectivation, everything was dull, beyond it, I am no longer as I was before, I am swept away by a becoming other, carried beyond my familiar existential Territories.

And this is not simply a gestalt configuration, crystallising the predominance of "good form." It's about something more dynamic, that I would prefer to situate in the register of the machine, as opposed to the mechanical. It is as biologists that Humberto Maturana and Francisco Varela proposed the concept of the autopoietic machine to define living systems. I think their notion of autopoiesis — as the auto-reproductive capacity of a structure or ecosystem — could be usefully enlarged to include social machines, economic machines and even the incorporeal machines of language, theory and aesthetic creation. Jazz, for example, is simultaneously nourished by its African genealogy and by its reactualisations in multiple and heterogeneous forms. As long as it is alive it will be like that. But like any autopoietic machine, it can die for want of sustenance or drift towards destinies which make it a stranger to itself.

Here then is an entity, an incorporeal ecosystem, whose being is not guaranteed from the outside; one which lives in symbiosis with the alterity it itself contributes to engendering; which is threatened with disappearance if its machinic essence is damaged by accident — the good and the bad encounters between jazz and rock — or when its enunciative consistency falls below a certain threshold. It is not an object "given" in extrinsic coordinates but an assemblage of subjectivation giving meaning and value to determinate existential Territories. This assemblage has to work in order to live, to processualise itself with the singularities which strike it. All this implies the idea of a necessary creative practice and even an ontological pragmatics. It is being's new ways of being which create rhythms, forms, colours and the intensities of dance. Nothing happens of itself. Everything has to continually begin again from zero, at the point of chaosmic emergence: the power of eternal return to the nascent state.

In the wake of Freud, Kleinian and Lacanian psychoanalysts apprehended, each in their own way, this type of entity in their fields of investigation. They christened it the "partial object," the "transitional object," situating it at the junction of a subjectivity and an alterity which are themselves partial and transitional. But they never removed it from a causalist, pulsional infrastructure; they never conferred it with the multivalent dimensions of an existential Territory or with a machinic creativity of boundless potential. Certainly, with his theory of the "objet a", Lacan had the merit of deterritorialising the notion of the object of desire. He defined it as non-specularisable, thus escaping the coordinates of space and time. He took it out of the limited field to which the post-Freudians had assigned it — the maternal breast, faeces and the penis — in order to relate it to the voice and the gaze. But he did not realise the consequences of his rupture with Freudian determinism, and didn't appropriately situate "desiring machines" — whose theory he had initiated — within incorporeal fields of virtuality. This object-subject of desire, like strange attractors in chaos theory, serves as an anchorage point within a phase space[1] (here, a Universe of reference) without ever being identical to itself, in permanent flight on a fractal line. In this respect it is not only fractal geometry that must be evoked, but fractal ontology. It is the being itself which transforms, buds, and transfigures itself. The objects of art and desire are apprehended within existential Territories which are at the same time the body proper, the self, the maternal body, lived space, refrains of the mother tongue, familiar faces, family lore, ethnicity.... No existential approach has priority over another. Thus it's not a question of a causal infrastructure and of a superstructure representative of the psyche, or of a world separated from sublimation. The flesh of sensation and the material of the sublime are inextricably interwoven. Relationship to the other does not proceed through identification with a preexisting icon, inherent to each individual. The image is carried by a becoming other, ramified in becoming animal, becoming plant, becoming machine and, on occasion, becoming human.

How can we, in this sensory submersion in a finite material, hold together an embodied composition (be it the most deterritorialised, as is the case with the material of music, or the material of conceptual art) and this hyper-complexity, this autopoiesis of aesthetic affects? In a compulsional manner — and here I return to that incessant coming-and-going between complexity and chaos. A cry, a monochrome blue, makes an

incorporeal, intensive, non-discursive, pathic Universe sudden-
ly appear, and as a result other Universes, other registers, other
machinic bifurcations are brought about: singular constellations of Universes. The most elaborate narratives, myths and
icons always return us to this point of chaosmic see-sawing, to
this singular ontological orality. Something is absorbed —
incorporated, digested — from which new lines of meaning
take shape and are drawn out. We had to pass through this
umbilical point — the white and greyish scabs at the back of
Irma's throat in Freud's principal dream or, by extension, an
object, fetishist and exorcising — so that a return to finitude
and precariousness could occur, to find a way out of eternal
and mortifying dreams, and to finally give back some infinity to
a world which threatened to smother it.

The blocks of sensation of machinic orality detach a deterritorialised flesh from the body. When I "consume" a work — a
term which ought to be changed, because it can just as easily
be absence of work — I carry out a complex ontological crystallisation, an alterification of beings-there. I summon being to
exist differently and I extort new intensities from it. Is it necessary to point out that such an ontological productivity in no
way leads to an alternative between Being and being or
between Being and nothingness? Not only is I an other, but it is
a multitude of modalities of alterity. Here we are no longer
floating in the Signifier, the Subject and the big Other in general. The heterogeneity of components (verbal, corporeal, spatial...) engenders an ontological heterogenesis all the more vertiginous when combined, as it is today, with the proliferation of
new materials, new electronic representations, and with a
shrinking of distances and an enlargement of points of view.
Informatic subjectivity distances us at high speed from the old
scriptural linearity. The time has come for hypertexts in every
genre, and even for a new cognitive and sensory writing that

Pierre Lévy describes as "dynamic ideography." Machinic mutations understood in the largest sense, which deterritorialise subjectivity, should no longer trigger in us defensive reflexes, backward-looking nervous twitches. It is absurd to impute to them the mass media stupefaction which four-fifths of humanity currently experience. It is simply a matter of the perverse counter-effect of a certain type of organisation of society, of the production and distribution of goods. Quite the contrary: the junction of informatics, telematics, and the audiovisual will perhaps allow a decisive step to be made in the direction of interactivity, towards a post-media era and, correlatively, an acceleration of the machinic return of orality. The era of the digital keyboard will soon be over; it is through speech that dialogue with machines will be initiated — not just with technical machines, but with machines of thought, sensation, and consultation.... All of this, I repeat, provided that society changes, provided that new social, political, aesthetic and analytical practices allow us to escape from the shackles of empty speech which crush us, from the erosion of meaning which is occurring everywhere (especially since the triumph of the spirit of capitalism in the Eastern bloc and the Gulf War).

Orality, morality! Making yourself machinic — aesthetic machine and molecular war machine (look at how important Rap culture is today for millions of young people) — can become a crucial instrument for subjective resingularisation and can generate other ways of perceiving the world, a new face on things, and even a different turn of events.

1   Abstract space where the axes represent the variables characterising the system.

6

The new aesthetic paradigm

It was only quite late in Western history that art detached itself
as a specific activity concerned with a particularised axiological
reference. Dance, music, the elaboration of plastic forms and
signs on the body, on objects and on the ground were, in archaic societies, intimately connected with ritual activities and religious representations. Equally, social relations, economic and
matrimonial exchanges, were, in the group life, hardly discernible from what I proposed calling territorialised
Assemblages of enunciation. Through diverse modes of semiotisation, systems of representation and multireferenced practices, these assemblages managed to crystallise complementary
segments of subjectivity. They released social alterity through
the union of filiation and alliance; they induced personal ontogenesis through the operation of peer groups and initiations,
such that individuals found themselves enveloped by a number
of transversal collective identities or, if one prefers, found themselves situated at the intersection of numerous vectors of partial
subjectivation. In these conditions, an individual's psychism
wasn't organised into interiorised faculties but was connected
to a range of expressive and practical registers in direct contact

with social life and the outside world. Such an interpenetration
of the socius with material activities and modes of semiotisation
leaves little place for a division and specialisation of work — the
notion of work itself remaining blurred — and, even less the
disengagement of an aesthetic sphere distinct from other
spheres (economic, social, religious or political).

It is not my intention to retrace, even summarily, the diverse
paths of deterritorialisation of these territorialised Assemblages
of enunciation. Let us just note that their general evolution will
move towards an accentuation of the individuation of subjectivity, towards a loss of its polyvocality — simply consider the
multiplication of names attributed to an individual in many
archaic societies — and towards an autonomisation of
Universes of value of the order of the divine, the good, the true,
the beautiful, of power.... This sectorisation of modes of valorisation is now so deeply rooted in the cognitive apprehension of
our era that it is difficult for us to trace its economy when we
try to decode past societies. How can we imagine, for example,
that a Renaissance prince did not buy works of art but attached
to himself masters whose fame reflected on his prestige.
Corporatist subjectivity with its pious implications for master
artisans of the Middle Ages who built the cathedrals remains
obscure to us. We cannot restrain ourselves from aesthetising a
rupestral art which, to all appearances, had an essentially technological and cultural significance. Thus any reading of the
past is inevitably overcoded by our references to the present.
Coming to terms with this does not mean that we should unify
fundamentally heterogeneous points of view. A few years ago
an exhibition in New York presented cubist works and productions of what is generally called primitive art side by side.
Formal, formalist and ultimately quite superficial correlations
were made, the two series of creations being detached from

their respective contexts — on the one side, tribal, ethnic, mythical; on the other, cultural, historical, economic. We shouldn't forget that the fascination that African, Oceanic and Indian art exercised on the cubists was not only of a plastic order but was associated with an exoticism of the period, informed by exploration, colonial expeditions, travel journals, adventure novels, whose aura of mystery was intensified by photography, cinema, sound recordings and by the development of field ethnology. If it is not illegitimate, and doubtless inevitable, to project onto the past the aesthetic paradigms of modernity, it can only be on the condition we recognise the relative and virtual character of the constellations of Universes of value brought about by this kind of recomposition.

Science, technology, philosophy, art and human affairs confront respectively the constraints and resistances of specific materials which they loosen and articulate within given limits. They do this with the help of codes, know-how and historical teachings which lead them to close certain doors and open other ones. The relations between the finite modes of these materials and the infinite attributes of the Universes of the possible they imply are different within each of these activities. Philosophy, for example, generates its own register of creative constraints, secretes its material of textual reference; it projects their finitude onto an infinite power corresponding to the auto-positioning and auto-consistency of its key concepts, at least at each mutant phase of its development. For their part, the paradigms of techno-science place the emphasis on an objectal world of relations and functions, systematically bracketing out subjective affects, such that the finite, the delimited and coordinatable, always takes precedence over the infinite and its virtual references. With art, on the contrary, the finitude of the sensible material becomes a support for the production of affects and percepts which tend to become more and more eccentred with respect to preformed structures and coordinates. Marcel Duchamp declared: "art is a road which leads towards regions which are not governed by time and space." The different domains of thought, action and sensibility position, in dissimilar ways, their movement from infinity into the passage of time, or rather into epochs capable of returning to or intersecting each other. For example, theology, philosophy and music today no longer compose a constellation as strong as during the Middle Ages. The metabolism of the infinite, proper to each assemblage, is not fixed once and for all. And when an important mutation appears within a domain, it can have "fallout," it can transversally contaminate many other domains (for example, the effect on the arts and literature of the potentially unlimited reproducibility of text and image by the printing press, or the power of cognitive transference acquired by mathematical algorithms in the sciences).

The aesthetic power of feeling, although equal in principle with the other powers of thinking philosophically, knowing scientifically, acting politically, seems on the verge of occupying a privileged position within the collective Assemblages of enunciation of our era. But before approaching this issue, it is necessary to further clarify its position within the anterior assemblages.

Let us return to the territorialised Assemblages of enunciation. Strictly speaking, they don't constitute a particular historical stage. Though they may characterise societies without writing or State, we can find relics or even active renaissances of them in developed capitalist societies — and without doubt they can be thought to hold a significant place in post-capitalist societies. Aspects of this kind of polysemic, animistic, transindividual subjectivity can equally be found in the worlds of infancy, madness, amorous passion and artistic creation. It might also be better here to speak of a proto-aesthetic paradigm, to emphasise that we are not referring to institutionalised art, to its works manifested in the social field, but to a dimension of creation in a nascent state, perpetually in advance of itself, its power of emergence subsuming the contingency and hazards of activities that bring immaterial Universes into being. A residual horizon of discursive time (time marked by social clocks), a perpetual duration, escapes the alternative of remembering-forgetting and lives with a stupefying intensity, the affect of territorialised subjectivity. Here the existential Territory becomes, at the same time, homeland, self-belonging, attachment to clan and cosmic effusion.

In this first illustration of an Assemblage, the category of space is in a position that can be described as globally aesthetised. Polyphonic spatial strata, often concentric, appear to attract and colonise all the levels of alterity that in other respects they engender. In relation to them, objects constitute themselves in a transversal, vibratory position, conferring on them a soul, a becoming ancestral, animal, vegetal, cosmic. These objectities-subjectities are led to work for themselves, to incarnate themselves as an animist nucleus; they overlap each other, and invade each other to become collective entities half-thing half-soul, half-man half-beast, machine and flux, matter and sign.... The stranger, the strange, evil alterity are dispelled into a menacing exterior. But the spheres of exteriority are not radically separated from the interior. Bad internal objects have to respond to everything governing the exterior worlds. In fact, there isn't really any exteriority: collective territorialised subjectivity is hegemonic; it folds one Universe of value into another in a general movement of folding over on itself. It gives rhythm to times and spaces at the pleasure of its interior tempo, its ritual refrains. The events of the macro-cosm are assimilated to those of the micro-cosm — to which they are also accountable. Space and time are thus never neutral receptacles; they must be accomplished, engendered by productions of subjectivity involving chants, dances, stories about ancestors and gods.... Here there is no effort bearing on material forms that does not bring forth immaterial entities. Inversely, every drive towards a deterritorialised infinity is accompanied by a movement of folding onto territorialised limits, correlative to a jouissance in the passage to the collective for-itself and its fusional and initiatory mysteries.

With deterritorialised assemblages, each sphere of valorisation erects a transcendent autonomised pole of reference: the Truth of logical idealities, the Good of moral will, the Law of public space, the Capital of economic exchangism, the Beautiful of the aesthetic domain.... This carving up of transcendence is consecutive to an individuation of subjectivity, which itself is divided up into modular faculties such as Reason, Understanding, Will, Affectivity.... The segmentation of the infinite movement of deterritorialisation is accompanied by a reterritorialisation, this time incorporeal: an immaterial reification. The valorisation which, in the preceding illustration, was polyphonic and rhizomatic, becomes bipolarised, Manicheanised, hierarchised and, in particularising its components, tends, in a certain way, to become sterilised. Dualisms in an impasse, like the oppositions between the sensible and the intelligible, thought and extensity, the real and the imaginary, involve a recourse to transcendent, omnipotent and homogenetic instances: God, Being, Absolute Spirit, Energy, The Signifier.... The old interdependence of territorialised values is thus lost, as are the experimentation, rituals and bricolages which led to their invocation and provocation — with the risk that they would reveal themselves as evanescent, dumb, without "surety" and even dangerous. Transcendent value presents itself as immovable, always already there and thus always going to stay there. From its perspective, subjectivity remains in perpetual lack, guilty a priori, or at the very least in a state of "unlimited procrastination" (following Kafka's expression in *The Trial*). The "lie of the ideal" as Nietzsche wrote, becomes "the curse on reality."[1] Thus modular subjectivity has no connection with the old dimension of the emergence of values which are neutralised under the weight of codes, rules and laws decreed by the transcendent enunciator. It is no longer the result of the changing contours of an intrication of spheres of valorisation secured to matters of expression — it is recomposed, as reified individuation, from Universals laid out according to an arborescent hierarchy. Imprescriptible laws, duties and norms take the place of the old prohibitions which always arranged a place for conjuration and transgression.

This sectorisation and bipolarisation of values can be defined as capitalistic due to the neutralisation, the systematic dequalification, of the materials of expression from which they proceed — which puts them into the orbit of the economic valorisation of Capital, treating as formally equal the values of desire, use values, exchange values, and which puts differential qualities and non-discursive intensities under the exclusive control of binary and linear relations. Subjectivity is standardised through a communication which evacuates as much as possible trans-semiotic and amodal enunciative compositions. Thus it slips towards the progressive effacement of polysemy, prosody, gesture, mimicry and posture, to the profit of a language rigorously subjected to scriptural machines and their mass media avatars. In its extreme contemporary forms it amounts to an exchange of information tokens calculable as bits and reproducible on computers. Modular individuation thus breaks up the complex overdeterminations between the old existential Territories in order to remodel the mental Faculties, a self, organs, personological, sexual and familial modalities of alterity, as so many pieces compatible with the mechanics of social domination. In this type of deterritorialised assemblage, the capitalist Signifier, as simulacrum of the imaginary of power, has the job of overcoding all the other Universes of value. Thus it extends to those who inhabit the domain of percept and aesthetic affect, who nevertheless remain — faced with the invasion of canonical redundancies and thanks to the precarious reopening of lines of flight from finite strata to incorporeal infinity — nuclei of resistance of resingularisation and heterogenesis.

Capitalistic deterritorialised Assemblages do not constitute well defined historical periods — any more than do emergent territorialised Assemblages. (Capitalistic drives are found at the heart of the Egyptian, Mesopotamian and Chinese empires, then throughout the whole of classical Antiquity.) The third type of processual Assemblage will be even more difficult to delimit, since it is only presented here prospectively, from traces and symptoms it appears to manifest today. Rather than marginalising the aesthetic paradigm, it confers on it a key position of transversality with respect to other Universes of value, from which it intensifies, each in its own way, creationist nuclei of autopoietic consistency. However, the end of the autarky and desertification of the Universes of value in the previous illustration is not synonymous with a return to the territorialised aggregation of emergent Assemblages. One does not fall back from the regime of reductionist transcendence onto the reterritorialisation of the movement of infinity in finite modes. The general (and relative) aesthetisation of the diverse Universes of value leads to a different type of re-enchantment of the expressive modalities of subjectivation. Magic, mystery and the demonic will no longer emanate, as before, from the same totemic aura. Existential Territories become diversified, heterogenised. The event is no longer enclosed in myth; it becomes a

nucleus of processual relay. The incessant clash of the movement of art against established boundaries (already there in the
Renaissance, but above all in the modern era), its propensity to
renew its materials of expression and the ontological texture of
the percepts and affects it promotes brings about if not a direct
contamination of other domains then at the least a highlight-
ing and a re-evaluation of the creative dimensions that traverse
all of them. Patently, art does not have a monopoly on creation, but it takes its capacity to invent mutant coordinates to
extremes: it engenders unprecedented, unforeseen and
unthinkable qualities of being. The decisive threshold constituting this new aesthetic paradigm lies in the aptitude of these
processes of creation to auto-affirm themselves as existential
nuclei, autopoietic machines. We can already sense the lifting
of shackles from the sciences constituted by the reference to a
transcendent Truth as the guarantee of its principle of consistency, which increasingly appears to relate to operational modelisations that stick as close as possible to immanent empiri-
cism. But in any event, whatever the detours of History, social
creativity seems called upon to expropriate its old rigid ideological structures, in particular those which served as a guarantee
of the eminence of State power and those which still make a
veritable religion out of the capitalist market. If we turn for a
moment to a discipline like psychoanalysis, which claimed to
affirm itself as scientific, it is increasingly clear that it has everything to gain from putting itself under the aegis of this new type
of aesthetic processual paradigm. Only in this way can it re-
acquire the creativity of its wild years at the turn of the century. Its vocation (depending on apparatuses, renewed procedures and references open to change) is to engender a subjectivity free from adaptive modelisations and capable of connect-
ing with the singularities and mutations of our era. We can
multiply the examples. In every domain we could find the same

interlacing of three tendencies: an ontological heterogenifica-
tion of Universes of reference deployed across what I have
called the movement of infinity; an abstract, machinic transversality articulating the multitudes of finite interfaces which
manifest these Universes in the same hypertext[2] or plane of
consistency; a multiplication and particularisation of nuclei of
autopoietic consistency (existential Territories). This processual
aesthetic paradigm works with (and is worked by) scientific
and ethical paradigms. It is installed transversally to techno-
science because technoscience's machinic Phylums are in
essence creative, and because this creativity tends to connect
with the creativity of the artistic process. But to establish such a
bridge, we have to shed our mechanist visions of the machine
and promote a conception which encompasses all of its aspects:
technological, biological, informatic, social, theoretical and
aesthetic. Once again, it is the aesthetic machine which seems
to be in the best position to disclose some of its often unrecognised but essential dimensions: the finitude relative to its life
and death, the production of proto-alterity in the register of its
environment and of its multiple implications, its incorporeal
genetic filiations.

   The new aesthetic paradigm has ethico-political implications because to speak of creation is to speak of the responsibility of the creative instance with regard to the thing created,
inflection of the state of things, bifurcation beyond pre-established schemas, once again taking into account the fate of
alterity in its extreme modalities. But this ethical choice no
longer emanates from a transcendent enunciation, a code of
law or a unique and all-powerful god. The genesis of enunciation is itself caught up in the movement of processual creation.
We see this clearly, with scientific enunciation, but always
with multiple heads: an individual head, of course, but also a
collective head, an institutional head, a machinic head with

experimental apparatuses, informatics, data banks, artificial
intelligence.... The process of differentiating these machinic
interfaces fragments the autopoietic enunciative nuclei and
renders them partial to the extent that it itself deploys itself
everywhere across the fields of virtuality of Universes of reference. But how, with this explosion of the individuation of the
subject and this fragmentation of interfaces, can we still speak
of Universes of value? No longer aggregated and territorialised
(as in the first illustration of Assemblage) or autonomised and
transcendentalised (as in the second), they are now crystallised
in singular and dynamic constellations which envelop and
make constant use of these two modes of subjective and
machinic production. One must never confuse here machinism
and mechanism. Machinism, in the way that I understand it,
implies a double process — autopoietic-creative and ethical-
ontological (the existence of a "material of choice") — which is
utterly foreign to mechanism. This is why the immense
machinic interconnectedness, the way the world consists
today, finds itself in an autofoundational position of its own
bringing into being. Being does not precede machinic essence;
the process precedes the heterogenesis of being.

Emergence tied to collective Territories, transcendent
Universals, processual Immanence: three modalities of praxis
and subjectivation specifying three types of enunciative
Assemblage involving equally the psyche, human societies, the
living world, machinic species and, in the last analysis, the
Cosmos itself. Such a "transversalist" enlargement of enunciation should lead to the fall of the "ontological Iron Curtain" (following Pierre Lévy's expression) that the philosophical tradi-
tion erected between mind and matter. The establishment of
such a transversalist bridge leads us to postulate the existence
of a certain type of entity inhabiting both domains, such that

the incorporeals of value and virtuality become endowed with an ontological depth equal to that of objects set in energetico-spatio-temporal coordinates. It is less a question of an identity of being which would traverse regions, retaining its heterogeneous texture, than of an identical processual persistence. Neither a Platonic Whole, nor an Aristotelian Prime Mover, these transversal entities appear like a machinic hyper-text — establishing themselves far beyond a simple, neutral support for forms and structures at the absolute horizon of all processes of creation. Thus one does not situate qualities or attributes as secondary in relation to being or substance; nor does one commence with being as a pure empty container (and a priori) of all the possible modalities of existing. Being is first auto-consistency, auto-affirmation, existence for-itself deploying particular relations of alterity. The for-itself and the for-others stop being the privilege of humanity; they crystallise everywhere that machinic interfaces engender disparity and, in return, are founded by it. The emphasis is no longer placed on Being — as general ontological equivalent, which, in the same way as other equivalents (Capital, Energy, Information, the Signifier) envelops, encloses and desingularises the process — it is placed on the manner of being, the machination producing the existent, the generative praxes of heterogeneity and complexity. The phenomenological apprehension of being existing as inert facticity only occurs in the case of limit experiences such as existential nausea or melancholic depression. Awareness of machinic being, on the other hand, will instead be deployed across multiple and polyphonic spatial and temporal envelopments and across potential, rational and sufficient developments in terms of algorithms, regularities and laws whose texture is just as real as its actual manifestations. And here once again emerges the thematic of virtual ecology and ecosophy.

The machinic entities which traverse these different registers of the actualised world and incorporeal Universes are two-faced like Janus. They exist concurrently in a discursive state within molar Fluxes, in a presuppositional relationship with a corpus of possible semiotic propositions, and in a non-discursive state within enunciative nuclei embodied in singular existential Territories, and in Universes of ontological reference which are non-dimensioned and non-coordinated in any extrinsic way.

How can we associate the non-discursive, infinite character of the texture of these incorporeals with the discursive finitude of energetico-spatio-temporal Fluxes and their propositional correlates? Pascal shows us a way in his response to the question: Do you think it is impossible that God is infinite and indivisible? "...I would like to show you something infinite and indivisible. It is a point which moves everywhere at infinite speed; because it is in all places and whole in each place."[3] In fact only an entity animated by an infinite speed (that is to say no longer respecting Einstein's cosmological limit of the speed of light) can hope to include both a limited referent and incorporeal fields of possibles and thereby give credibility and consistency to the contradictory terms of a proposition. But with this Pascalian speed deploying an "infinite and indivisible thing" we are still only left with an ontologically homogeneous infinity, passive and undifferentiated. The creativity intrinsic to the new aesthetic paradigm demands more active and activating folds of this infinity, in two modalities, which we will now examine, whose double articulation is characteristic of the machine in the wider sense envisaged here.

An initial chaosmic folding consists in making the powers of chaos co-exist with those of the highest complexity. It is by a continuous coming-and-going at an infinite speed that the multiplicities of entities differentiate into ontologically heterogeneous complexions and become chaotised in abolishing their figural diversity and by homogenising themselves within the same being-non-being. In a way, they never stop diving into an umbilical chaotic zone where they lose their extrinsic references and coordinates, but from where they can re-emerge invested with new charges of complexity. It is during this chaosmic folding that an interface is installed —an interface between the sensible finitude of existential Territories and the trans-sensible infinitude of the Universes of reference bound to them. Thus one oscillates, on one hand, between a finite world of reduced speed, where limits always loom up behind limits, constraints behind constraints, systems of coordinates behind other systems of coordinates, without ever arriving at the ultimate tangent of a being-matter which recedes everywhere and, on the other hand, Universes of infinite speed where being can't be denied anymore, where it gives itself in its intrinsic differences, in its heterogenetic qualities. The machine, every species of machine, is always at the junction of the finite and infinite, at this point of negotiation between complexity and chaos.

These two types of ontological consistency — heterogenetic being-quality and homogenetic being-matter-nothingness — do not involve any Manichean dualism, since they constitute themselves from the same plane of entitative immanence and envelop each other. But the price to pay for this initial level of immanence and complexity is that it does not deliver the key to the stabilisation, localisation and rhythmisation of decelerating chaosmic stases and strata, of "freeze framings" of complexity, of what prevents the latter from turning back and from once again being swallowed up by chaos and of what leads them, on the contrary, to engender limits, regularities, constraints, laws, and everything that the second autopoietic folding must assume.

In fact, it is not legitimate to try to intercept finite contingency on such a direct route between chaos and complexity. There are two reasons for this. On one hand, the fleeting complexion which emerges from chaos to return there at infinite speed is itself the virtual bearer of reduced speeds. On the other, the chaosmic umbilicus, insofar as it develops consistency, also has a role to play in the birth of finitude with its two functions of existential grasping and transmonadism. Thus, we will be led to superpose the immanence of infinity and finitude onto the immanence of complexity and chaos; we will have to assume that the primordial slowing down manifested in finite speeds, proper to limits and extrinsic coordinates and to the promotion of particularised points of view, inhabits chaos just as much as the infinite entitative speeds which attempt to domesticate philosophy with their conceptual creations. The movement of infinite virtuality of incorporeal complexions carries in itself the possible manifestation of all the components and all the enunciative assemblages actualisable in finitude. So chaosmosis does not oscillate mechanically between zero and infinity, being and nothingness, order and disorder: it rebounds and irrupts on states of things, bodies and the autopoietic nuclei it uses as a support for deterritorialisation; it is relative chaotisation in the confrontation with heterogeneous states of complexity. Here we are dealing with an infinity of virtual entities infinitely rich in possibles, infinitely enrichable through creative processes. It is a force for seizing the creative potentiality at the root of sensible finitude — "before" it is applied to works, philosophical concepts, scientific functions and mental and social objects — which founds the new aesthetic paradigm. The potentiality of the event-advent of limited speeds at the heart of infinite speeds constitutes the latter as creative intensities. Infinite speeds are loaded with finite speeds, with a conversion of the virtual into the possible, of the reversible into irreversible, of the deferred into difference. The same entitative multiplicities constitute virtual Universes and possible worlds; this potentiality of finite, sensible bifurcation inscribed in an irreversible temporality remains in an absolute, reciprocal presupposition with a-temporal reversibility, the incorporeal eternal return of infinitude.

A throw of dice
Never
Even indeed when thrown in eternal circumstances

From the depths of a shipwreck...

This irruption of the irreversible, these choices of finitude can only be framed — so as to acquire a relative consistency — on condition that they are inscribed on a memory of being and positioned in relation to axes of ordination and reference. The autopoietic fold responds to these two demands by putting into action its two inextricably associated facets of appropriation (or existential grasping) and trans-monadic inscription. But the grasping only confers auto-consistency on the monad to the extent that it deploys a transmonadic exteriority and alterity such that neither the first nor second benefit from a relation of precedence, and that one cannot approach either of them without referring to the other.

Let us nevertheless start with the grasping side: it establishes a "holding together" between:
— the respective autonomy of the complexion and its chaosmic umbilicus, their distinction, their absolute separation;
— and their equally absolute concatenation, within the same plane of double immanence.

Our experience of such ambivalent positioning and fusional abolition is given through the apprehension of Kleinian partial objects — the breast, faeces, the penis...which crystallise the self even as they dissolve it in projective-introjective relations with the other and with the Cosmos. An incorporeal complexion, snatched up by grasping, will only receive its character of finitude if the advent-event of its encounter with a transmonadic line occurs, which will trigger the exit, the expulsion of its infinite speed, its primordial deceleration. Before this crossing of the threshold, the existence of the incorporeal complexion, just as much as that of the composition and of the assemblage — candidates for actualisation — remains aleatory and evanescent. The complex entitative multiplicity is only indexed by an autopoietic nucleus. Here, we evoke the experience of earliest dream recollection with the wild flight of its traits of complexity. Everything really begins when transmonadism enters the scene to inscribe and transform this first autopoietic coupling. We too must start again from its side.

The permanent metabolism of nihilation, the depolarisation and dissipation of the diverse that shapes the monad, prevents it from delimiting a distinctive identity. The fusional nothing of a "given" monad inhabits the nothing of another monad and so on to infinity, in a course of multidirectional relays with stroboscopic resonances. How does such a trail of nihilation, at once omnipotent and impotent, come to be the means of inscription for a reappearance of finitude, how does it become deterritorialisation? It is because where there was only infinite disappearance, absolute dispersion, the transmonadic slide introduces an ordered linearity — one moves from one point of consistency to another — thereby allowing the ordination of incorporeal complexions to crystallise. Chaosmosis functions here like the pickup head of a Turing machine. The chaotic nothing spins and unwinds complexity, puts it in relation with itself and with what is other to it, with what alters it. This actu-

alisation of difference carries out an aggregative selection onto
which limits, constants and states of things can graft themselves. Already we are no longer at the speeds of infinite dissolution. There is something left over, a remainder, the selective
erection of semblances and dissemblances. In symbiosis with
infinite complexions, finite compositions insert themselves
within extrinsic coordinates, enunciative assemblages fit
together in relations of alterity. Linearity, the matrix of all ordination, is already a slowing down, an existential stickiness. It
might seem paradoxical that it is the persistence of a nihilation
— or rather of an intensive deterritorialisation — which gives
its corporeal consistency to autopoietic states of things and
points of view. But only this type of linear and rhizomatic distancing can select, arrange and proportion a complexity which
will now live under the double regime of a discursive slowing
down and of an absolute speed of non-separability. The virtual
complexion which has been selected is then stamped with an
irreversible facticity enveloped by a proto-temporality that can
be described as instantaneous and eternal and easily recognised in the phenomenological apprehension of Universes of
value. Transmonadism through the effect of retro-activity crystallises within the primitive chaotic soup spatial coordinates,
temporal causalities, energy levels, possibilities for the meeting
of complexions, a whole ontological "sexuality" composed by
axiological bifurcations and mutations. In this way, the second
fold of autopoietic ordination — intensely active and creationist — separates from the inherent passivity of the first chaosmic
fold. The passivity will transform itself into a limit, a framing, a
sensitive refrain out of which an enrichment of finite and "controlled" complexity can emerge — while ontological heterogeneity will transform itself into alterity. Nothing will work
until such an event-advent of primordial slowing-down and
selection has happened — from the moment it is inscribed on

the transmonadic, autopoietic network. Such an aleatory limit of a virtual point of view becomes a necessary and sufficient accident in the extraction of a fold of contingency, or a "choice" of finitude. From now on we have to make do with it, start from there, return to it and circle around.

Through this precipitation of crystals of finitude and this declination of attractors of the possible, the limits of territorialisation will be irremediably promoted — limits such as those of relativity and of photon exchange, of regularities and constraints; limits like that of a quantum of action, limits that scientific assemblages will semiotise into functions, constants and laws. But the decisive point remains that the transmonadic breakout, far from resolving itself on the fixed horizon of nihilation, curls up along an infinite twisting line of flight whose circumvolutions, like those of strange attractors, give chaos a consistency at the intersection of the actualisation of finite configurations and an always possible processual recharge — the medium for ordinal and novel bifurcations, for energetic conversions escaping the entropy of territorialised stratifications — and open to the creation of mutant assemblages of enunciation.

It is a striving towards this ontological root of creativity that is characteristic of the new processual paradigm. It engages the composition of enunciative assemblages actualising the compossibility of two infinities, the active and the passive. A striving that is in no way constrained, catatonic or abstract like those of capitalistic monotheisms, but animated by a mutant creationism, always to be re-invented, always about to be lost. The irreversibility belonging to the events-advents of autopoietic grasping and transmonadism is consubstantial with a permanent resistance to circular, reterritorialising repetitions and with a constant renewal of aesthetic boundaries, scientific apparatuses of partial observation, philosophical conceptual montages and the establishment of "habitats" (*oikos*) that are political or psychoanalytical (ecosophy). To produce new infinities from a submersion in sensible finitude, infinities not only charged with virtuality but with potentialities actualisable in given situations, circumventing or dissociating oneself from the Universals itemised by traditional arts, philosophy, and psychoanalysis: all things that imply the permanent promotion of different enunciative assemblages, different semiotic recourses, an alterity grasped at the point of its emergence — non- xenophobic, non-racist, non-phallocratic — intensive and processual becomings, a new love of the unknown.... In the end, a politics and ethics of singularity, breaking with consensus, the infantile "reassurance" distilled by dominant subjectivity. Dogmatisms of every kind investing and obscuring these points of creationism, points which necessitate a permanent confrontation (in the analysis of the unconscious as in all the other disciplines) with the collapsus of non-sense, with insoluble contradictions — the manifestations of short-circuits between complexity and chaos. For example, the democratic chaos which conceals a multitude of vectors of resingularisation, attractors of social creativity in search of actualisation. No question here of aleatory neo-liberalism with its fanaticism for the market economy, for a univocal market, for a market of redundancies of capitalist power, but of a heterogenesis of systems of valorisation and the spawning of new social, artistic and analytical practices.

So the question of inter-monadic transversality is not simply of a speculative nature. It involves calling into question disciplinary boundaries, the solipsistic closure of Universes of value, prevalent today in a number of domains. Let us take as a final example an open redefinition of the body, so necessary for the promotion of therapeutic assemblages of psychosis: the body conceived as intersection of partial autopoietic components, with multiple and changing configurations, working collectively as well as individually; all "the bodies" — the specular body, the fantasmatic body, the neurological corporeal schema, the biological and organic soma, the immune self,[4] the personological identity within familial and environmental eco-systems, collective faciality, refrains (mythical, religious, ideological...) So many existential territorialities linked by the same transversal chaosmosis, so many monadic "points of view" terraced or structured across fractal ascents and descents, authorising a combined strategy of analytical approaches (institutional psychotherapeutic, psychopharmalogical) and personal recomposition that is either delirious or of an aesthetic character.... It is one and the same thing to declare these territories partial and yet open to the most diverse fields of alterity: this clarifies how the most autistic enclosure can be in direct contact with ambient social constellations and the machinic Unconscious, historical complexes and cosmic aporias.

1   Friedrich Nietzsche, *Ecce Homo*, trans. W. Kaufmann, Vintage, New York, 1989, p. 218.
2   Cf. Pierre Lévy, op. cit.
3   Pascal, *Pensées*, trans. A.J. Krailsheimer, Penguin, Harmondsworth, 1968, p.153.
4   Anne-Marie Moulin, *Le dernier langage de la médecine. Histoire de l'immunologie de Pasteur au sida*, PUF, Paris, 1991.

7

The ecosophic object

Geopolitical configurations are changing at a great pace whilst the Universes of technoscience, biology, computer technology, telematics and the media further destabilise our mental coordinates on a daily basis. The suffering of the Third World, demographic cancer, the monstrous growth and degradation of the urban fabric, the insidious destruction of the biosphere by pollution and the incapacity of the system to reconstruct a social economy adapted to the new technologies — all of this ought to lead to the mobilisation of minds, sensibilities and wills. But the acceleration of a history, which might lead us to ruin, is masked by the sensationalist (in fact banalising and infantilising) imagery that the media concoct from current events.

The ecological crisis can be traced to a more general crisis of the social, political and existential. The problem involves a type of revolution of mentalities whereby they cease investing in a certain kind of development, based on a productivism that has lost all human finality. Thus the issue returns with insistence: how do we change mentalities, how do we reinvent social practices that would give back to humanity — if it ever had it — a sense of responsibility, not only for its own survival, but equally for the future of all life on the planet, for animal and vegetable species, likewise for incorporeal species such as music, the arts, cinema, the relation with time, love and compassion for others, the feeling of fusion at the heart of cosmos?

It is certainly worthwhile reconstituting collective means of communication and action appropriate to a historical situation which has radically devalued old ideologies, social practices and traditional politics. In this respect, we should note that it is entirely possible that the new communication technologies will contribute to a renewal of similar means of elaboration and intervention. But it is not these, as such, that will trigger creative sparks, that will engender pockets of awareness capable of deploying constructive perspectives. New collective assemblages of enunciation are beginning to form an identity out of fragmentary ventures, at times risky initiatives, trial and error experiments; different ways of seeing and of making the world, different ways of being and of bringing to light modalities of being will open up, be irrigated and enrich one another. It is less a question of having access to novel cognitive spheres than of apprehending and creating, in pathic modes, mutant existential virtualities.

To recognise subjective factors in History and the leap of ethical liberty involved in advancing a genuine virtual ecology in no way implies withdrawal into oneself (as in transcendental meditation) or a renunciation of political engagement. It requires, on the contrary, a refoundation of political praxis.

Since the end of the Eighteenth century, the impact of science and technology on developed societies has been accompanied by an ideological, social and political bipolarisation between progressive currents — often Jacobinist in their understanding of the State — and conservative currents advocating a fixation on traditional values. It was in the name of the Enlightenment, liberty, progress, then of the emancipation of the workers, that a left-right axis was established as a kind of basic reference.

Today, the social-democracies have been converted if not to liberalism then at least to the primacy of the market economy, whilst the generalised collapse of the international communist movement has left a gaping hole in one of the extremes of this bipolarity. In these conditions, should we imagine that the bipolarity ought to disappear, as the slogan of some ecologists would have it: "neither left, nor right"? Wouldn't it be the social itself which will be effaced, like an illusion, as certain adherents of post-modernism have affirmed? As opposed to these positions, I consider that progressivist polarisation ought to be reconstituted through more complex schemas, according to less Jacobinist modalities, more federalist, more dissensual, in relation to which the different mixtures of conservatism, centrism, even neo-fascism, would be repositioned. The traditional party formations are too enmeshed with the different wheels of the State for systems of parliamentary democracy to disappear overnight. And this despite their obvious loss of credibility, expressed by a growing disaffection of the electorate, as well as by a flagrant lack of conviction on the part of those citizens who do continue to vote. Political, social and economic stakes are increasingly rare in electoral battles — which most of the time are no more than large mass media manoeuvres. A certain form of "politics for politicians" seems destined to be eclipsed by a new type of social practice better suited both to issues of a very local nature and to the global problems of our era.

The masses of the Eastern bloc threw themselves into a kind of collective chaosmosis in order to free themselves from totalitarianism, to live differently — fascinated as they were by Western models. But it is becoming increasingly evident that the failure of "socialism" is also an indirect failure of the allegedly liberal regimes which lived in hot or cold symbiosis with it for decades. Failure in the sense that Integrated World Capitalism — though it has managed to guarantee sustained economic growth in most of its citadels (at the cost, it's true, of considerable ecological devastation and ferocious segregation) — is not only incapable of releasing Third World countries from their impoverishment, but also because it has nothing to offer other than very partial answers to the huge problems assailing the Eastern bloc and the USSR, thus exacerbating the bloody inter-ethnic ordeals from which there currently appears to be no way out.

An expanded ecological consciousness going far beyond the electoral influence of the "Greens" should in principle lead to putting the ideology of production for the sake of production back into question, that is, production centred on profit in the capitalist context of cost structure and debilitating consumerism. The objective would no longer be to simply take control of State power in place of the reigning bourgeoisie and bureaucracy, but to determine with precision what one intends to put in their place. In this respect, it seems to me that two complementary thematics should come to the forefront in future debates on the recomposition of a progressivist cartography:
— the redefinition of the State, or rather of State functions which are in reality multiple, heterogeneous and often contradictory;
— the deconstruction of the concept of the market and the recentering of economic activities on the production of subjectivity.

Bureaucratisation, sclerosis, the slide of State machines towards totalitarianism do not only concern the Eastern bloc but also Western democracies and Third World countries. The withering away of State power, once advocated by Rosa Luxemburg and Lenin, is more relevant than ever. The com-

munist movement brought discredit on itself — and to a lesser
extent so did the social-democrats — for having been incapable
of struggling effectively against the ravages of State control in
every domain; the parties laying claim to these ideologies having become themselves, with the passage of time, appendages
of State apparatuses. Nationalistic questions are re-emerging in
the worst subjective conditions (nationalism, uniformity,
racial hatred...) since no appropriate federalist response has
been advanced as an alternative to an abstract and fictitious
internationalism.

The neo-liberal myth of the world market has acquired incredi-
ble powers of suggestion over the last few years. According to
this myth, no sooner does an economic ensemble submit to its
law than its problems dissolve as if by magic. The African States
which haven't been able to enter this market are condemned to
vegetate economically and to beg for international assistance.
A State like Brazil, where resistance by the oppressed continues, is destabilised in its relation to the world economy and by
hyper-inflation; while countries like Chile and Argentina,
which are subject to the monetarist controls of the IMF, have
only been able to tame inflation and stabilise their finances by
plunging 80% of their populations into unimaginable misery.

   In fact, a hegemonic world market does not exist, but only
sector-based markets corresponding to so many power formations. The financial market, the oil market, the real estate mar-
ket, the armaments market, the drug market, the NGO market,
etc., have neither the same structure nor the same ontological
texture. They only adjust to one another through the relations
of forces established between the power formations which sus-
tain them. Today a new ecological power formation is appearing under our noses and, consecutively, a new ecological
industry is in the process of making a place for itself within

other capitalist markets. The systems of heterogenetic valorisation — which counterbalance capitalist homogenesis rather than passively contesting the ravages of the world market — have to put in place their own power formations which will affirm themselves within new relations of forces. Artistic assemblages, for example, will have to organise themselves so as not to be delivered, bound hand and foot, to a financial market itself in symbiosis with the drug market. The education market cannot remain absolutely dependent on the State market. Markets valorising a new quality of urban life and post-mass media communication will have to be invented. Exploding the hegemony of the capitalist valorisation of the world market consists in giving consistency to the Universes of value of social assemblages and existential Territories which situate themselves, in a manner of speaking, against the implosive evolution we are witnessing.

In order to counteract reductionist approaches to subjectivity, we have proposed an analysis of complexity starting with an ecosophic object with four dimensions:
— material, energetic and semiotic Fluxes;
— concrete and abstract machinic Phylums;
— virtual Universes of value;
— finite existential Territories.
    The ecosystemic approach of Fluxes still represents an indispensable awareness of the cybernetic interaction and feedback involved with living organisms and social structures. But it is as much a matter of establishing a transversalist bridge between the ensemble of ontological strata which, each in their own way, are characterised by specific figures of chaosmosis. Here one is thinking of the visibilised and actualised strata of material and energetic Fluxes, of the strata of organic life, of those of the Socius, of the mecanosphere, but also of the incor-

poreal Universes of music, of mathematical idealities, of
Becomings of desire.... Transversality never given as "already
there," but always to be conquered through a pragmatics of
existence. Within each of these strata, each of these Becomings
and Universes what is put into question is a certain metabolism
of the infinite, a threat of transcendence, a politics of immanence. And, each one of them will require schizoanalytic and
ecosophic cartographies which will demand that partial components of enunciation be brought to light where they exist but
are unrecognised and where scientism, dogmatism and tech-
nocracy prevent their emergence. Thus chaosmosis does not
presuppose an invariant composition of the four ontological
dimensions of Fluxes, Territories, Universes and machinic
Phylums. It has no pre-established schemas, as is the case with
the universal figures of catastrophe in René Thom's theory. Its
cartographic representation forms part of a process of existential production involving territorialised components of finitude,
irreversible embodiment, processual singularity and the engendering of Universes of virtuality which are not directly locatable
within extrinsic discursive coordinates. They come to being
through an ontological heterogenesis and affirm themselves
within the world of significations as a rupture of sense and existential reiteration. The positionality of these refrains in the
ordinary world will be effected, for example, as a derivative and
a-signifying function of mythical, literary, fantasmatic and ...
theoretical narrativity.

   The theoretical discourses of Marxism and Freudianism
which claimed to be solidly constructed on scientific diagram-
matics only found their social affirmation to the extent that
they themselves catalysed such nuclei of partial subjectivation.
Our own attempt at meta-modelising enunciation, based on
existential Territories and incorporeal Universes obviously cannot avoid the impossibility of its direct objective representation.

Simply, our theoretical refrain would be more deterritorialised than current representations of the Unconscious, structure, system.... Grasping the non-discursive dimension of enunciation and the necessary articulation between complexity and chaos led us to advance the concept of a pre-objectal entity as an element in the ontological texture, transversal to Fluxes, machinic Phylums, Universes of value and existential Territories — the being [*l'être*] before being [*être*] now conceived from a multicomponential and intensive perspective. The entity animated by infinite velocity dissolves the categories of time and space and consequently even the notion of speed. From the intensity of its slowing down the categories of the object, of the delimited set and of partial subjectivation can be deduced. The chaosmic fold of deterritorialisation and the autopoietic fold of enunciation, with their interface of existential grasping and transmonadism, implant at the heart of the object-subject relation — and before any instance of representation — a creative processuality, an ontological responsibility which binds liberty and its ethical vertigo at the heart of ecosystemic necessities.[1]

To speak of machines rather than drives, Fluxes rather than libido, existential Territories rather than the instances of the self and of transference, incorporeal Universes rather than unconscious complexes and sublimation, chaosmic entities rather than signifiers — fitting ontological dimensions together in a circular manner rather than dividing the world up into infrastructure and superstructure — may not simply be a matter of vocabulary! Conceptual tools open and close fields of the possible, they catalyse Universes of virtuality. Their pragmatic fallout is often unforeseeable, distant and different. Who knows what will be taken up by others, for other uses, or what bifurcations they will lead to!

The activity of cartography and ecosophic metamodelisation, where being becomes the ultimate object of a heterogenesis under the aegis of a new aesthetic paradigm, should be at the same time more modest and more audacious than the conceptual productions to which the University has accustomed us. More modest in renouncing any pretension to durability or eternal scientific authority, and more audacious in taking sides in the extraordinary sprint currently occurring between machinic mutations and their subjective "capitalisation." Engagement in innovative social, aesthetic and analytical practices is thus correlative to crossing the threshold of intensity of speculative imagination, coming not only from specialised theoreticians, but also from assemblages of enunciation confronted with the chaosmic transversality proper to the complexity of ecosophic objects. And opening up ethico-political options that relate as much to the microscopic aspects of the psyche and socius as to the global destiny of the biosphere and mecanosphere from now on calls for a permanent reappraisal of the ontological foundations of existing modes of valorisation in every domain.

This cartographic activity can incarnate itself in multiple ways. A distorted foreshadowing is presented to us by the psychoanalytic or family therapy session, the reunions of institutional analysis, professional networking, socio-professional or neighbourhood collectives.... The common characteristic of all these practices appears to be verbal expression. Today the psyche, the couple, the family, neighbourhood life, the school, the relation with time and space, with animal life, sounds, plastic forms — everything has to be put back into the position of being spoken. Yet the ecosophic (or schizoanalytic) approach is not confined to the level of verbal expression alone. Of course Speech remains an essential medium, but it's not the only one; everything which short-circuits significational chains, postures, facial traits, spatial dispositions, rhythms, a-signifying semiotic productions (relating, for example, to monetary exchange), machinic sign productions, can be implicated in this type of analytical assemblage. Speech itself — and I could never overemphasise this — only intervenes here inasmuch as it acts as a support for existential refrains.

The primary purpose of ecosophic cartography is thus not to signify and communicate but to produce assemblages of enunciation capable of capturing the points of singularity of a situation. In this perspective, meetings of a political or cultural character will have the vocation of becoming analytical and, inversely, psychoanalytical work will have to gain a foothold in multiple micropolitical registers. Like the symptom for Freudianism, the rupture of sense, the dissensus, becomes a privileged primary material. "Personal problems" should be able to irrupt on the private or public scene of ecosophic enunciation. In this respect, it is striking to notice how the French ecological movement, in its diverse components, has shown itself to be incapable of dealing with basic issues. It is completely dedicated to a discourse of an environmental or political nature. If you ask ecologists what they intend to do to help the homeless in their suburb, they generally reply that it's not their responsibility. If you ask them how they intend to free themselves from a certain dogmatism and the practices of small groups, many of them will recognise that the question is well-founded, but are quite unable to suggest any solutions! When in truth their problem today is not how to keep themselves at an equal distance from the left and the right, but how to contribute to the reinvention of progressivist polarity, how to rebuild politics on different bases, how to rearticulate transversally the public and the private, the social, the environmental and the mental. In order to move in this direction, new types of dialogue, of analysis, of organisation will have to be tested; perhaps at first on a small scale then later on a larger one. If the ecological movement in France today, which appears to have so much promise, fails to engage with this problem of recomposing militant situations (in an entirely new sense, that is to say, of collective assemblages of subjectivation) then it will certainly lose the capital of confidence invested in it, and the technical and associative aspects of ecology will be recuperated by the traditional parties, State power and eco-business. To my mind, the ecological movement should concern itself, as a matter of priority, with its own social and mental ecology.

In France, certain intellectual leaders were traditionally invested with the mission of guiding opinion. Happily this period seems to be over. After having experienced the reign of the intellectuals of transcendence — the prophets of existentialism, "organic" intellectuals (in Gramsci's sense) of the great militant era, then, closer to us, the preachers of the "moral generation" — perhaps we will now have to come to terms with an immanence of collective intellectuality, one that penetrates the world of teachers, social workers, and technical milieux of every description. Too often the promotion of leading intellectuals by the media and publishing houses has had the effect of inhibiting the inventiveness of collective Assemblages of intellectuality which in no way benefit from such a system of representation. Intellectual and artistic creativity, like new social practices, have to conquer a democratic affirmation which preserves their specificity and right to singularity. This being the case, intellectuals and artists have got nothing to teach anyone. To return to an image that I proposed a long time ago, they produce toolkits composed of concepts, percepts and affects, which diverse publics will use at their convenience. As for morality, it has to be admitted that a pedagogy of values does not exist. The Universes of the beautiful, the true and the good are inseparable from territorialised practices of expres-

sion. Values only have universal significance to the extent that
they are supported by the Territories of practice, experience, of
intensive power that transversalise them. It is because values
are not fixed in a heaven of transcendent Ideas that they can
just as easily implode, attaching themselves to catastrophic
chaosmic stases. Le Pen has become a dominant object of the
collective libido — either to elect or reject him — due to his skill
in attracting media attention but principally because of the
weakening of the existential Territories of subjectivity of what
is called the left — the progressive loss of its heterogenetic values relating to its internationalism, antiracism, solidarity, innovative social practices.... Be that as it may, intellectuals should
no longer be asked to erect themselves as master thinkers or
providers of moral lessons, but to work, even in the most
extreme solitude, at putting into circulation tools for transversality.

Artistic cartographies have always been an essential element of the framework of every society. But since becoming the
work of specialised corporate bodies, they may have appeared
to be side issues, a supplement of the soul, a fragile superstructure whose death is regularly announced. And yet from the
grottoes of Lascaux to Soho taking in the dawn of the cathedrals, they have never stopped being a vital element in the crystallisation of individual and collective subjectivities.

Fabricated in the socius, art, however, is only sustained by
itself. This is because each work produced possesses a double
finality: to insert itself into a social network which will either
appropriate or reject it, and to celebrate, once again, the
Universe of art as such, precisely because it is always in danger
of collapsing.

What confers it with this perennial possibility of eclipse is its
function of rupturing with forms and significations circulating

trivially in the social field. The artist — and more generally aesthetic perception — detach and deterritorialise a segment of the real in such a way as to make it play the role of a partial enunciator. Art confers a function of sense and alterity to a subset of the perceived world. The consequence of this quasi-animistic speech effect of a work of art is that the subjectivity of the artist and the "consumer" is reshaped. In short, it is a matter of rarefying an enunciation which has too great a tendency to become entangled in an identificatory seriality which infantilises and annihilates it. The work of art, for those who use it, is an activity of unframing, of rupturing sense, of baroque proliferation or extreme impoverishment, which leads to a recreation and a reinvention of the subject itself. A new existential support will oscillate on the work of art, based on a double register of reterritorialisation (refrain function) and resingularisation. The event of its encounter can irreversibly date the course of an existence and generate fields of the possible "far from the equilibria" of everyday life.

Viewed from the angle of this existential function — namely, in rupture with signification and denotation — ordinary aesthetic categorisations lose a large part of their relevance. Reference to "free figuration," "abstraction," or "conceptualism" hardly matters! What is important is to know if a work leads effectively to a mutant production of enunciation. The focus of artistic activity always remains a surplus-value of subjectivity or, in other terms, the bringing to light of a negentropy at the heart of the banality of the environment — the consistency of subjectivity only being maintained by self-renewal through a minimal, individual or collective, resingularisation.

The growth in artistic consumption we have witnessed in recent years should be placed, nevertheless, in relation to the increasing uniformity of the life of individuals in the urban context. It should be emphasised that the quasi-vitaminic function of this artistic consumption is not univocal. It can move in a direction parallel to uniformisation, or play the role of an operator in the bifurcation of subjectivity (this ambivalence is particularly evident in the influence of rock culture). This is the dilemma every artist has to confront: "to go with the flow," as advocated, for example, by the Transavantgarde and the apostles of postmodernism, or to work for the renewal of aesthetic practices relayed by other innovative segments of the Socius, at the risk of encountering incomprehension and of being isolated by the majority of people.

Of course, it's not at all clear how one can claim to hold creative singularity and potential social mutations together. And it has to be admitted that the contemporary Socius hardly lends itself to experimentation with this kind of aesthetic and ethico-political transversality. It nonetheless remains the case that the immense crisis sweeping the planet — chronic unemployment, ecological devastation, deregulation of modes of valorisation, uniquely based on profit or State assistance — open the field up to a different deployment of aesthetic components. It doesn't simply involve occupying the free time of the unemployed and "marginalised" in community centres! In fact it is the very productions of science, technology and social relations which will drift towards aesthetic paradigms. It's enough to refer to the latest book by Ilya Prigogine and Isabelle Stengers where they evoke the necessity of introducing into physics a "narrative element" as indispensable to a genuine conception of evolution.[2]

Today our societies have their backs up against the wall; to survive they will have to develop research, innovation and creation still further — the very dimensions which imply an awareness of the strictly aesthetic techniques of rupture and suture. Something is detached and starts to work for itself, just

as it can work for you if you can "agglomerate" yourself to
such a process. Such requestioning concerns every institutional domain, for example, the school. How do you make a class
operate like a work of art? What are the possible paths to its singularisation, the source of a "purchase on existence" for the
children who compose it?[3] And on the register of what I once
called "molecular revolutions," the Third World conceals trea-
sures which deserve to be explored.[4]

    A systematic rejection of subjectivity in the name of a myth-
ical scientific objectivity continues to reign in the University. In
the heyday of structuralism the subject was methodically
excluded from its own multiple and heterogeneous material of
expression. It is time to re-examine machinic productions of
images, signs of artificial intelligence, etc., as new materials of
subjectivity. In the Middle Ages, art and technique found
refuge in the monasteries and convents which had managed to
survive. Perhaps artists today constitute the final lines along
which primordial existential questions are folded. How are the
new fields of the possible going to be fitted out? How are sounds
and forms going to be arranged so that the subjectivity adjacent to them remains in movement, and really alive?
    The future of contemporary subjectivity is not to live indefi-
nitely under the regime of self-withdrawal, of mass mediatic
infantilisation, of ignorance of difference and alterity — both
on the human and the cosmic register. Its modes of subjectivation will get out of their homogenetic "entrapment" only if creative objectives appear within their reach. What is at stake here
is the finality of the ensemble of human activities. Beyond
material and political demands, what emerges is an aspiration
for individual and collective reappropriation of the production
of subjectivity. In this way the ontological heterogenesis of
value becomes the focus of political concerns which at present

lack the site, the immediate relation, the environment, the reconstitution of the social fabric and existential impact of art.... And at the end of a slow recomposition of assemblages of subjectivation, the chaosmic explorations of an ecosophy — articulating between them scientific, political, environmental and mental ecologies — ought to be able to claim to replace the old ideologies which abusively sectorised the social, the private and the civil, and which were fundamentally incapable of establishing transversal junctions between the political, the ethical and the aesthetic.

It should, however, be clear that we are in no way advocating an aesthetisation of the Socius, for after all, promoting a new aesthetic paradigm involves overthrowing current forms of art as much as those of social life! I hold out my hand to the future. My approach will be marked by mechanical confidence or creative uncertainty, according to whether I consider everything to be worked out in advance or everything to be there for the taking — that the world can be rebuilt from other Universes of value and that other existential Territories should be constructed towards this end. The immense ordeals which the planet is going through — such as the suffocation of its atmosphere — involve changes in production, ways of living and axes of value. The demographic explosion which will, in a few decades, see the population of Latin America multiply by three and that of Africa by five[5] does not proceed from an inexorable biological malediction. The key factors in it are economic (that is, they relate to power) and in the final analysis are subjective — cultural, social and mass mediatic. The future of the Third World rests primarily on its capacity to recapture its own processes of subjectivation in the context of a social fabric in the process of desertification. (In Brazil, for example, Wild West capitalism, savage gang and police violence coexist with interesting attempts by the Workers' Party movement at recomposing social and urbanistic practices.)

Among the fogs and miasmas which obscure our *fin de millénaire*, the question of subjectivity is now returning as a leitmotiv. It is not a natural given any more than air or water. How do we produce it, capture it, enrich it, and permanently reinvent it in a way that renders it compatible with Universes of mutant value? How do we work for its liberation, that is, for its resingularisation? Psychoanalysis, institutional analysis, film, literature, poetry, innovative pedagogies, town planning and architecture — all the disciplines will have to combine their creativity to ward off the ordeals of barbarism, the mental implosion and chaosmic spasms looming on the horizon, and transform them into riches and unforeseen pleasures, the promises of which, for all that, are all too tangible.

1 On the ethical obligation towards a "progeny", cf. Hans Jonas, *The Imperative of Responsibility*, University of Chicago Press, Chicago,1984.
2 "For mankind today, the 'Big Bang' and the evolution of the Universe are part of the world in the same way as in prior times, the myths of origin," in *Entre le temps et l'éternité*, Fayard, 1988, p.65.
3 Among the many works on institutional pedagogy, see René Lafitte, *Une journée dans une classe coopérative: le désir retrouvé*, Syros, Paris, 1985.
4 On the networks of solidarity subsisting amongst those "defeated" by modernity in the Third World: Serge Latouche, *La Planète des naufragés. Essai sur l'après-développement*, La Découverte, 1991.
5 Jacques Vallin (de l'INED), *Transversales Science/Culture*, Number 9, June, 1991. (29 rue Marsoulan, 75012 Paris). *La population mondiale, la population française*, La Découverte, Paris, 1991.